Praise for
Biohacking for the Sales Athlete

"Everyone wants an edge, but most people are looking in the wrong places. At the highest level, performance isn't just about how hard you train, it's about how well you recover. What Nicole is doing translates that same mindset into the business world. If you want to perform like an elite athlete, you have to live like one."

—Bronson Kaufusi, former NFL Player,
Harris Investment Group, OG1 Athlete Advisor

"Nicole understands something many leaders overlook: the nervous system is the foundation of performance. In Biohacking for the Sales Athlete, she translates emerging science around recovery, stress regulation, and physiology into practical tools for people operating at the highest levels of business."

—Anna Gudmundson,
CEO, Sensate

"Nicole helped me think about health the way high performers should: as a foundation for leadership and decision-making. By applying some of the nutrition and performance strategies she recommends, I experienced meaningful changes in my sleep, energy, and overall well-being. The impact on my professional life was immediate."

—Arthi Chakravarthy,
Chief Legal Officer, Enovix

"*Strategy gets you to the table. Your nervous system determines what happens when you sit down. Nicole Ward wrote the book on both.*"

—Olga Gvozdenovic,
Dual-sport Division 1 athlete, Duke University,
Founder, OMG Basketball Academy

"*Top performers in business train for results, but very few train their physiology. Nicole's work reframes performance through the lens of health optimization.* Biohacking for the Sales Athlete *shows how leaders can think about recovery, energy, and resilience the way elite athletes do. It's a powerful framework for anyone responsible for driving outcomes at a high level.*"

—Jeff Benton,
Founder and CEO, Paragon

BIOHACKING

for the

SALES

ATHLETE

OPTIMIZE YOUR HEALTH TO TRANSFORM YOUR RESULTS

NICOLE ELIZABETH WARD

The information contained in this book is for educational and informational purposes only and is not intended as medical advice, diagnosis, or treatment. The author is not a physician and does not provide medical services or prescribe treatment.

The content presented reflects the author's professional experience, research, and personal observations in the fields of performance optimization, health coaching, nutrition, and leadership development. It is not a substitute for individualized medical care or advice from a qualified healthcare professional.

Readers should consult their physician or other qualified healthcare provider before beginning any new health, nutrition, supplementation, exercise, or biohacking protocol, particularly if they have existing medical conditions, are pregnant or nursing, or are taking medications.

The use of any information provided in this book is solely at the reader's own risk. The author and publisher disclaim any liability for any direct or indirect loss, injury, or damage arising from the application of the information contained herein.

For the ugly ducklings. The late bloomers.
Transformation has no deadline.

Table of Contents

FOREWORD
Coherent Power

At the highest level, this work is not really about sales. It isn't even, fundamentally, about health. It is about restoring coherence between power and consciousness.

Modern society has concentrated extraordinary power—financial, technological, political, cultural—into the hands, minds, and nervous systems of a relatively small group of people. Executives, founders, board members, investors, dealmakers, decision-makers. People whose choices ripple outward into markets, organizations, families, and communities.

Yet the biology carrying that power is often anything but coherent.

These people are chronically overstimulated. Sleep-deprived. Inflamed. Running on caffeine, cortisol, adrenaline, and willpower. Living in a constant low-grade state of fight-or-flight while being asked to make long-term, ethical, high-stakes decisions.

That mismatch is not benign.

When nervous systems are dysregulated, we see it everywhere:

- Decisions become short-term.
- Risk skews toward either fear or recklessness.
- Creativity collapses into reactivity.
- Presence erodes.
- Listening narrows.
- Ethics quietly thin at the edges.

Power without regulation distorts. Power without coherence fragments. Power without embodied awareness becomes dangerous—not necessarily in dramatic ways, but in subtle, cumulative ones that shape cultures, policies, and lives downstream.

I believe the nervous system is the hidden infrastructure of leadership.

Before strategy, before vision, before culture, before performance, there is state. The state of the body. The tone of the autonomic nervous system. The coherence between heart, brain, and breath. The capacity to stay grounded under pressure, to remain open rather than defensive, to sense clearly rather than react blindly.

This is where biohacking enters the conversation—not as a vanity pursuit of optimization, not as Silicon Valley longevity cosplay, but as something far more consequential:

- Biohacking as the applied science of self-regulation
- Biohacking as nervous-system literacy
- Biohacking as the technology of coherence

At its best, biohacking is not about chasing more—more productivity, more years, more metrics. It is about alignment. About restoring the body's ability to move fluidly between activation and recovery, focus and rest, drive and discernment. It is about creating the physiological conditions for clarity, presence, emotional intelligence, and ethical decision-making.

It is about bringing power back into the right relationship with the body that carries it.

This is the foundation of what I call the Executive Athlete.

An Executive Athlete is not simply a high performer who works out. It is a leader who trains their nervous system with the same intentionality that elite athletes train their bodies. They understand that:

- Recovery is a performance strategy, not a luxury.
- Regulation is a leadership skill, not a personality trait.
- Presence is physiological before it is psychological.
- Energy, focus, intuition, and resilience are biological capacities that can be trained, measured, and restored.

They recognize that their state—both physical and mental—shapes their impact. That every room they walk into, every decision they make, every conversation they lead is influenced—often invisibly—by their internal coherence or lack thereof.

My mission with the Executive Athlete is to help high-impact humans come back into the right relationship with themselves: with their bodies, their breath, their intuition, their energy, and their responsibility. To move from brute force to embodied power. From chronic overdrive to sustainable clarity. From fragmented performance to integrated presence.

This book is my most practical entry point into that mission. And it begins, intentionally, in the arena where pressure is constant, stakes are personal, rejection is frequent, and performance is publicly measured: Sales.

Sales was my first proving ground. It is a crucible of nervous-system stress: quotas, competition, travel, time zones, sleep disruption, social drinking, cognitive load, emotional labor, and the relentless requirement to be "on."

If someone can learn to regulate their physiology in that proving ground—protect their energy, stabilize their focus, recover quickly, and lead themselves under pressure—the skills translate everywhere. Into boardrooms. Into leadership teams. Into relationships. Into decision-making under uncertainty. Into how capital is stewarded, how people are managed, how risk is assessed, and how futures are shaped.

> I believe the nervous system is the hidden infrastructure of leadership.

The Sales Athlete[1] is not separate from the Executive Athlete. It is the training ground, and my own initiation into this work did not come through theory. It came through my body.

Abruptly.

Violently.

Unmistakably.

It came the day my nervous system finally forced me to stop.

---

[1] Sales Athlete™ is a registered trademark of Nicole Elizabeth Ward.

INTRODUCTION
The Sales Crucible

Sales is where performance meets pressure in real time.

It is where nervous systems are tested daily by uncertainty, rejection, competition, travel, time zones, social demands, quotas, and the constant requirement to be "on." It is where cognition, emotional regulation, energy, and resilience are not theoretical concepts, but survival skills. And it is where the cost of dysregulation shows up quickly: in burnout, brain fog, poor decisions, reactive communication, compromised health, strained relationships, and shortened careers.

Over the course of my twenty-five-year career in sales and executive leadership, I have lived nearly every statistic associated with stress, overwork, and burnout. Sales professionals are significantly more likely than the general workforce to report anxiety, depression, sleep deprivation, circadian disruption from travel, social over-drinking, and an inability to sustain true work-life balance. I didn't need a research report to tell me that. I was the data.

I have lost sleep.

I have lived on airplanes and in hotel rooms.

I have over-consumed, over-networked, and over-extended.

I have passed up family events and personal milestones in the name of quotas and closing cycles.

I have woken up in cities I couldn't immediately place.

I have confused adrenaline for drive and cortisol for commitment.

Like many high achievers, I was successful on paper long before I was coherent in my body.

Sales is often described as a marathon, but in reality, it is a series of repeated sprints with insufficient recovery in between. Back-to-back meetings. Back-to-back flights. Back-to-back quarters. Back-to-back expectations. The sympathetic nervous system rarely gets a break. Over time, this creates a state of chronic activation that masquerades as ambition but slowly erodes clarity, creativity, intuition, sleep, immunity, hormonal balance, and emotional regulation.

And yet, in sales, we rarely talk about the physiology of performance.

- We talk about tactics.
- We talk about pipelines.
- We talk about playbooks, CRMs, productivity systems, time blocking, and closing frameworks.

What we don't talk about is the state of the nervous system that is executing all of it.

- What happens when a leader is exhausted but still making decisions that affect people's livelihoods?

- What happens when a sales professional is inflamed, sleep-deprived, and cognitively depleted, yet expected to build trust, read subtle cues, and influence outcomes?
- What happens when ambition outpaces regulation?

This is the crucible.

Sales is the environment where the gap between biological capacity and performance demand becomes impossible to ignore. When your cognition is off, your pitch suffers. When your energy crashes, your follow-up falters. When your sleep is fragmented, your emotional regulation thins. When your nervous system is in threat mode, your ability to connect, influence, and read the room collapses.

No CRM can fix that. No script can compensate for it. No productivity hack can override biology.

This is where biohacking becomes not a luxury but a necessity. Biohacking, as I use the term in this book, is not about gadgets or gimmicks. It is about understanding and working with your biology instead of against it. It is about learning how your nervous system responds to stress, travel, food, light, alcohol, sleep, hormones, and emotional load, and then using that data to make precise, strategic changes that restore coherence.

Biohacking is the applied science of self-regulation.

When you optimize sleep, stabilize blood sugar, support mitochondrial function, regulate inflammation, balance neurotransmitters, and train your vagus nerve, you are not just improving health metrics. You are upgrading your decision-making, emotional intelligence, presence, and resilience under pressure. You are increasing your capacity to stay grounded when stakes are high, to listen when tension is present, to respond rather than react, and to lead with clarity instead of survival chemistry.

This is the foundation of the Sales Athlete.

A Sales Athlete understands that their body is not separate from their performance. That their nervous system is their most important piece of equipment. That recovery is not weakness, but strategy. That coherence is the hidden edge.

> Bio-hacking is about making small, deliberate changes to your lifestyle that yield significant improvements in energy, focus, resilience, recovery, and overall well-being.

Professional athletes would never compete chronically sleep-deprived, inflamed, under-recovered, and under-nourished. Yet in the business world, this is normalized. Even celebrated. Hustle culture has taught us to override biological signals in the name of output. The result is a population of high-achieving, high-earning, high-impact professionals quietly running on dysregulated systems.

The cost shows up everywhere: in burnout, in stalled careers, in health crises, in lost clarity, in strained relationships, and in the slow erosion of joy and purpose.

Sales was my first arena for this work. The Executive Athlete is the larger identity it revealed.

For me, the wake-up call didn't come from a spreadsheet or a quarterly review, but from my body itself. And that moment would become the doorway into everything that followed.

The research now confirms what so many of us in sales have felt in our bones for years. Sales professionals are significantly more likely than the general workforce to experience anxiety and depression. Burnout rates are dramatically higher. Sleep is shorter and more fragmented. Circadian rhythms are routinely disrupted by travel across time zones. Social drinking is normalized and often professionally reinforced. And only a small minority report anything resembling true work-life balance.

Sales is often described as a marathon, but in reality, it is a series of high-stakes sprints. Quotas reset. Pipelines refill. Presentations stack. Travel compresses. Pressure rarely lets up. With all of these competing demands, it is easy to lose sight of the most critical element of success: the state of the body and brain doing the work.

Imagine walking into a client meeting with the same clarity, confidence, and nervous-system steadiness as a professional athlete stepping onto the field. You are sharp. You are focused. You are emotionally regulated. You are fully present. That is the promise of the Sales Athlete.

Peak health is not about aesthetics. It is about capacity. It is about cognitive endurance, emotional resilience, and the ability to perform under sustained pressure. This is where traditional productivity methods fall short.

Time-blocking, pipeline management, CRMs, and sales enablement tools can help you work more efficiently, but they do nothing to address the underlying state of the system doing the work. When you are physically depleted, emotionally dysregulated, and neurologically overtaxed, no calendar hack or email template can compensate. Every Sales Athlete is different. The beauty of biohacking is that it is customizable. Whether you are a road warrior crossing time zones weekly or a leader running back-to-back virtual meetings all day, the principles are the same: stabilize the biology, and performance follows.

I saw this truth crystallize in one of my own team members. Several years ago, I managed a sales director named Yvette. She was smart, connected, motivated, and talented. On paper, she had everything she needed to succeed. In reality, she was chronically overextended. She was attending too many events, drinking too much at client dinners, sleeping poorly, and constantly running on depleted reserves. Her performance suffered, not because she lacked skill, but because her nervous system and recovery were compromised.

We made a few simple changes. Fewer late nights. A limit on alcohol. Better sleep support. Strategic supplementation. More recovery. Within a week, her clarity returned. Her energy stabilized. Her confidence rose. Within a month, her results shifted dramatically.

Nothing about her intelligence changed. Nothing about her talent changed.

Her physiology did.

That is the leverage point.

That is the Sales Athlete mindset.

Professional athletes do not hope their bodies will hold up under pressure. They train them to. They respect recovery as much as effort. They understand that performance is built in the margins: in sleep, nutrition, nervous-system regulation, and consistency.

As a sales professional, your game day is every day. Your brain is your primary instrument. Your nervous system is your performance engine. Your energy, focus, emotional regulation, and resilience determine how you show up in rooms where trust, influence, and opportunity are created.

The stakes are not just personal. They are professional and financial.

- Have you ever missed a deal because you were foggy, flat, or reactive in a critical meeting?
- Have you ever lost momentum because your energy crashed when it mattered most?
- Have you ever been overlooked for an opportunity because you were operating below your cognitive and emotional best?

Your health is not separate from your results. It is a direct driver of them.

What You Can Expect from This Book

This is not a book about selling tactics.

This is not a traditional nutrition manual.

This is a practical, science-backed guide to optimizing the system that sells.

You will learn how to:

- Stabilize your energy across long days and heavy travel.
- Improve sleep and recovery even with demanding schedules.
- Regulate stress and nervous-system reactivity.
- Fuel your brain for clarity, confidence, and presence.
- Use simple biohacks and wearables to personalize your performance.
- Build resilience that sustains success, not just sprints toward it.

Each chapter will give you tools you can apply immediately—small adjustments that create meaningful shifts in how you feel, think, and perform.

Ready to Compete?

Whether you are a senior sales executive leading global teams or a rep fighting to break into the top tier, there is always another level of performance available when the body and brain are aligned.

This book is your invitation to train like the athlete you already are. Not just to work harder. Not just to hustle more. But to operate from a regulated, resilient, high-performing nervous system that can meet pressure with clarity and power.

The question is not whether sales is demanding. The question is whether you are ready to meet those demands with a system trained to win.

Let's begin.

The Sales Buddha's Corner
Sit in the Fire

We are whole organisms, a compilation of systems whose sum is greater than its parts. As important as it is to look individually at our diet, mental health, emotional well-being, performance ... the truth is that everything is connected. If we have a problem, health challenge, or struggle in one area, it's highly likely that it's connected to other things—or an even deeper cause.

As sales professionals, it's often the case that we are moving at a fast pace, and when issues or challenges arise, we want to solve them fast and move on. In those scenarios, it's easy to gloss over what's really going on for us emotionally or physically. I challenge you to *not* do that. Instead, see the struggle or issue as an opportunity to lean into what's causing you to slow down. Take a closer look. It's often uncomfortable, and we can want to resist—but it's where the real learning comes in. Whether it's an internal process within your company, an ongoing communication challenge with a colleague, or a particularly difficult client—if it's bothering you, it's telling you there's something there that can be learned. As one of my gurus, Peter Crone, says, "Our triggers in life show us where we are not free."

The end of each chapter of this book will have one of these "The Sales Buddha's Corner" features to give you an opportunity to pause and contemplate how your contributing "parts" of health, performance, and personal circumstances are all connected and greater than their "sum."

How Did I Get Here?

I didn't set out to become a biohacker, a performance optimizer, or someone who could speak fluently about cortisol curves, circadian rhythms, mitochondrial health, or nervous system regulation. I certainly didn't imagine that one day I'd be teaching high-performing sales leaders how to think about their bodies the same way elite athletes do.

I started with a degree in Cultural Anthropology from UC Santa Barbara, a deep curiosity about people and behavior, and absolutely no idea how I was going to translate that into paying rent.

When a recruiting firm called Brewer Personnel offered me a job, I said yes without hesitation. The hours were brutal. I was in the office by 7:00 a.m. and rarely left before 9:00 p.m. The environment was competitive, fast, and relentlessly metrics-driven. And I was good at it. Really good.

Within a few years I was leading teams, managing fifteen people while still in my twenties, hitting numbers, winning accounts, and being rewarded with more responsibility, more pressure, and more expectations. From the outside, it looked like success. From the inside, something very different was happening.

I was gaining weight rapidly—nearly forty pounds in a short span of time. I remember standing in our bullpen one day and joking with my team that maybe my dry cleaner was shrinking my clothes. I'm not sure how they managed to keep straight faces.

My days were spent sitting. My fuel consisted of artificially sweetened coffee, powdered creamer, and whatever highly processed "healthy-sounding" option the business park café offered. Meals were inhaled at my desk between calls. Work came first. Sleep, movement, nourishment, and any semblance of balance came last.

Like many ambitious young professionals, I believed that success required sacrifice. And my body was the sacrifice.

When I finally started to notice how disconnected I felt from myself physically, I did what most people do. I tried to "work out more" and "eat better," without any real understanding of what that meant. There was no conversation about bio-individuality, no awareness of macronutrient balance, no discussion of circadian alignment or nervous system recovery. There was simply a cultural mantra: burn more calories.

My choice to become a vegetarian in college only added to the imbalance. Information about how to be a truly well-nourished vegetarian in the 1990s was practically nonexistent. Think pasta, bread, and frozen veggie burgers marketed as health food. Protein was an afterthought. Blood sugar stability wasn't a concept. Eating late at night after long workdays and client dinners was the norm.

Alcohol was part of the culture. Heavy meals at 8:00 or 9:00 p.m., followed by poor sleep and groggy mornings, were standard operating procedure.

I didn't yet have the language for what was happening in my body, but I was living with the consequences: fragmented sleep, low energy, brain fog, and a constant sense of running on fumes. Today, I would recognize the signs immediately: dysregulated cortisol, poor heart rate variability, disrupted REM and deep sleep, and a nervous system that never truly downshifted out of "on."

The moment I can now clearly label as my first true wake-up call came in a conference room, on a Tuesday afternoon, across the table from a CFO we were close to closing.

I nodded off.

Not metaphorically. Literally.

I have no idea if the prospect or my colleague noticed, but I did. The realization landed like a punch to the chest. I was so exhausted, so out of sync with my body, that I couldn't even maintain alertness in a high-stakes meeting that directly affected my career and my team. The weight gain, the poor sleep, the constant stimulation and depletion were no longer cosmetic or inconvenient. They were now interfering with performance.

My body was trying to get my attention.

It did so again, much more dramatically, not long after.

I was driving between offices, rushing as usual, juggling back-to-back calls, proud of myself for being "efficient." I had left my house before dawn to make an early team meeting in San Jose, then jumped in the car to head to Pleasanton for an 11:00 a.m. appointment, trying to squeeze in as much as possible before leaving that weekend for an eighteen-day vacation to Greece and Turkey. I was burned out, overstretched, and operating in a constant state of sympathetic overdrive, although I didn't yet have the vocabulary to describe it that way.

My new Land Rover had Bluetooth, which at the time felt like cutting-edge technology. Hands-free, multitasking, always on. I was on a call when another driver, intent on making an exit, cut across four lanes of traffic.

The impact was violent. Metal screamed against pavement. The world tilted. The vehicle lifted, rolled, and spun. In a matter of seconds, my car was on its side, the sound of grinding steel still echoing in my ears.

They say your life flashes before your eyes. What I remember most clearly is that sound. And then, incredibly, my first conscious thought was not about my body, or the other driver, or the fact that my car was destroyed.

It was: I have to get to the office. Where is my phone?

I climbed out through the passenger window once the electronics allowed it, work bag in hand. I noticed my left hand swelling rapidly. The airbag had broken two fingers, though I wouldn't fully process that until later. My suit was immaculate. My hair and makeup were intact. Fifty yards away, the other vehicle lay on its side as well.

I was so far out of tune with my body that I could not maintain focus or stay awake, so far out of tune with my life that I put the career I valued so greatly at risk.

I called 911. Then, while waiting for emergency responders, I called my boss.

"I've been in an accident. I'm not going to make the eleven o'clock meeting."

To his credit, he told me to forget the meeting, go to the hospital, go home, and pour myself a glass of scotch.

That contrast stayed with me. My nervous system was so conditioned to prioritize performance and productivity that even a rollover accident barely interrupted the internal script of obligation.

This was not resilience. This was dysregulation disguised as dedication.

The accident became a line in the sand. A moment I could no longer rationalize away. The financial success, the travel, the beautiful homes and cars had all come at a cost. By my late thirties, it was clear that I had optimized for achievement while systematically depleting the very systems that allowed achievement in the first place: my body, my brain, my nervous system.

Not long after, a former colleague who had left the corporate world to become a personal trainer re-entered my life. She had transformed herself completely. Sixty pounds lost. Muscle built. Energy restored. At fourteen years my senior, she radiated vitality. Her example was undeniable proof that decline was not inevitable and that the body was not a liability to be managed, but an asset to be trained.

She gave me a small calorie book and told me to highlight everything I ate. The exercise was humbling. Between training sessions, a gym membership, and a newfound awareness of intake, I lost forty-two pounds in seven months.

But something still wasn't right.

I was thinner, but not optimized. Lighter, but not truly well. The dress size changed. The underlying physiology had not yet caught up.

And that realization marked the true beginning of what would become a fifteen-year journey into performance science, longevity, nervous system regulation, and what I now call becoming a Sales Athlete.

The weight loss was a milestone, but it wasn't the destination. I had changed my appearance, but I hadn't yet changed my operating system.

I was still exhausted. Still wired and tired. Still riding waves of energy crashes in the afternoon and staring at the ceiling at night, mind racing, body unable to fully drop into restoration. I didn't yet understand the role of macronutrient balance, blood sugar stability, nervous system tone, or hormonal signaling. I was doing what many high performers do: solving the visible problem while ignoring the invisible infrastructure that made sustainable performance possible.

At the same time, I began to notice something more subtle but equally corrosive. Despite my success, despite the promotions and commission checks and external validation, I carried a persistent sense that I didn't quite belong in the rooms I was in. Impostor syndrome whispered constantly. Maybe I was lucky. Maybe I had just been in the right place at the right time. Maybe someone would eventually figure out that I wasn't as sharp or as capable as I appeared.

The lifestyle of sales amplified that internal narrative. Poor sleep, frequent travel, late nights, alcohol-fueled client dinners, and early-morning meetings are a perfect recipe for cognitive dulling and emotional volatility. Brain fog became familiar. Mornings after late-night work events felt like wading through wet cement. In meetings, I sometimes hesitated to speak, not because I lacked insight, but because I didn't fully trust the clarity of my own thinking. When your nervous system is chronically overstimulated and under-recovered, confidence erodes from the inside out.

I was thin, but I was miserable.

Sales is not an eight-to-five profession. It is a vocation that lives in the margins of the day. Breakfast meetings at dawn. Full days of presentations and negotiations. Evening events with clients. Calls that span time zones. Weekend texts. Emergency travel when something goes wrong. The very traits that make great sales leaders successful—responsiveness, service orientation, emotional attunement, availability—also keep the nervous system in a near-constant state of activation.

Over time, that "always on" state takes a physiological toll. Elevated cortisol. Disrupted circadian rhythms. Suppressed deep sleep. Inflammation. Insulin resistance. The slow erosion of mitochondrial efficiency. At the time, I didn't have the language for any of this. I only knew that something fundamental was off.

As my curiosity about health deepened, it became an obsession in the best sense of the word. I devoured podcasts, medical journals, and books on longevity, metabolism, neuroscience, and performance. I sought out functional medicine physicians and longevity clinics. I invested in labs that traditional healthcare rarely covers. I tracked biomarkers, hormones, inflammatory markers, nutrient levels, and genetic predispositions. I learned how differently men and women respond to fasting and training across the lifespan. I began using wearables to correlate what I ate, when I ate, how I slept, how I trained, and how my nervous system responded.

I tested. I adjusted. I experimented. I failed forward.

I learned that not all calories are equal. That macronutrient ratios matter profoundly for cognitive function and hormonal balance. That alcohol, even in moderate amounts, dramatically alters sleep architecture. That eating late at night suppresses melatonin and growth hormone. That inflammation and gut health influence mood, motivation, and mental clarity. That stress is not just a psychological experience but a biochemical cascade that shapes everything from fat storage to memory formation.

Slowly, the fog lifted.

Energy stabilized. Sleep deepened. Focus sharpened. Emotional resilience increased. The sense of being an impostor began to loosen its grip, not because external achievements changed, but because my internal state did. A regulated nervous system thinks more clearly, tolerates uncertainty more gracefully, and shows up with a kind of grounded confidence that cannot be faked.

What I came to understand is this: performance is biological before it is psychological. You cannot out-mindset a dysregulated system. You cannot out-hustle depleted mitochondria. You cannot will your way into clarity when your brain is under-fueled, under-slept, and swimming in stress hormones.

Fifteen years ago, we didn't have the tools we have now. We didn't have continuous glucose monitors, Oura

Rings, or Apple Watches providing real-time feedback. We didn't routinely test for heavy metals, mold exposure, or gut permeability. We didn't talk about the microbiome, epigenetics, or the female-specific nuances of metabolic health and training. Today, the landscape is entirely different. The data exists. The science exists. The opportunity to optimize, rather than merely survive, is unprecedented.

And that is why this book exists.

Not because everyone needs to become a biohacker in the extreme sense, but because every high-performing professional deserves to understand the physiology that underpins their performance. Sales is a cognitive sport. Leadership is a nervous-system sport. Decision-making, emotional regulation, creativity, persuasion, and presence all emerge from the state of the body.

When your biology is supported, your psychology follows.

The Sales Buddha's Corner
Wheel of Life

Imagine your life as a wheel, with each spoke representing a domain: health, career, relationships, finances, family, social life, creativity, spirituality, recovery, play. When you allow yourself to pause and truly reflect, how balanced is your life wheel? When all spokes are relatively even, the wheel turns smoothly. When one or two dominate while others wither, the ride becomes unstable.

Early in my career, my wheel was wildly out of balance. Career and achievement were overdeveloped spokes. Health, recovery, and presence were barely there. I was pushing, fixing, solving, producing, and performing, but rarely pausing long enough to notice the cost.

As a Gen-Xer raised with grit and a strong work ethic, I knew how to work hard. What I didn't know how to do was apply that same discipline to nourishment, recovery, and self-regulation. I wanted the easy button when it came to health. Minimal input, maximal output. Life eventually taught me what every athlete learns: there is no shortcut around the fundamentals.

Resistance is not the enemy. It is the doorway. The places in your life that feel most uncomfortable to look at are often the ones that hold the greatest potential for growth. Hedonic choices promise immediate pleasure. Eudaimonic choices build long-term vitality, meaning, and capacity.

As you move through this book, I invite you to examine your own wheel. Where are the gaps? Where are the imbalances? Where might you be choosing short-term relief over long-term resilience?

Optimization is not about perfection. It is about alignment. About choosing, again and again, the behaviors that move you closer to the summit you are trying to climb. And giving yourself permission to pause, to listen, and to recalibrate before your body is forced to deliver its message in a language as loud as mine once did.

2

Facelift

S ales is in desperate need of a facelift. I've spent my career as a sales executive evangelizing the value of sales in the face of pervasive, never-ending, belittling discounting of what we do for a living. But the stereotypes of "the world's second oldest profession" and "used car salesman" persist. It's exhausting. I'm not saying that there isn't a small percentage of our fellow sales professionals who fulfill this stereotype, but for most of us these clichés don't reflect our motivation or our reality.

I continue to hold an aspirational view of sales and the integrity of our profession. Ultimately, sales is *service*. For many of us, selling becomes an honor and a privilege, giving us the opportunity to support and offer our company's resources to a network of people we genuinely grow to value and care for. I stand committed to giving sales a "rebrand" and using the mind-body connection to health and wellness as the path to do it. Just because we have quotas to hit and can be money-motivated doesn't mean we don't do the right thing when no one is looking. When we are at our best mentally, physically, and soulfully, there's no chance to be seen as "slick" or "sales-y," because we're coming from a grounded and healthy place that demonstrates a higher commitment and purpose beyond immediate personal gain. By taking better holistic care of ourselves as sales executives, we could do a great deal to dispel the derogatory views and opinions surrounding our profession.

Yet the demands on the sales professional and the lifestyle often required of us can be taxing. For those outside of sales, our lifestyles look quite the opposite of demanding—fancy dinners, high-end happy hours, golf outings, travel to desirable locations for conferences and trade shows. Acquaintances often envy our lifestyle, at least the lifestyle they think they see. But as sales professionals, we know their view is inaccurate or at least wildly incomplete. We know all too well the reality others don't see: late nights entertaining, over-drinking and over-eating; constant movement between time zones with resulting jet lag and temporal displacement; the unfamiliar transitory nature of sleeping in different hotels every night; inconsistent workout routines; time away from family and friends; the constant demands of being with clients during workdays that usually extend into after-work evenings and breakfast meetings … generally a lifestyle that is anything but glamorous *or* healthy.

In my experience, most of my colleagues didn't graduate from college with a master plan to go into sales. Like me, it's something that happened … by default, accident, necessity, or ambition. Sales can be a way to carve a better, more lucrative livelihood for ourselves. Most of the sales professionals I know come from modest upbringings, and sales afforded (literally) an opportunity to leapfrog our past circumstances. I'm not alone. Consider just a few comments from sales professionals posting on Reddit:[2]

- "Sales is the best 'low skill' career where a person can go from not having a penny in their name to becoming a 1% income earner. … Don't get offended by the use of 'low skill' in my post. I'm simply referring to the amount of training and education needed for the entry point into a profession."
- "Sales can serve as a career path for individuals from lower socioeconomic backgrounds, offering opportunities for significant income growth."
- "My parents raised me in a Habitat for Humanity $40k home. Free college with a state grant and grinding in restaurants. I just moved my mother into my $615k home to live with my wife, twins, and I."
- "When I was twenty-four, I started out with nothing. $40,000 in college debt. No family help. But I had one significant goal in mind. I wanted to find a sales position that would give me a good foundation and allow me to move up to financial stability. I had no family support and no mentors guiding me. I had a college degree, bartending and serving experience, that was about it. In my first sales position, I made less than

---

[2] https://www.reddit.com/r/sales/comments/mxbk0y/sales_is_the_path_out_of_poverty_and_the_middle/

the guy at McDonald's. It was strictly commissioned with a draw. It was a great foundation with a very reputable company. A year later, it led me to the next step: a move to another company where I was finally able to pay my bills and get my own apartment. A year later, another step with a major legal publishing company propelled me down the six-figure path. When I was twenty-seven, I paid off $30,000 in debt with one commission check, which was the remaining balance."

Here are some sales demographic statistics from Xactly and DataUSA.io:

- Gender Distribution in Sales: 33.1 percent women, 66.9 percent men
- Sales Occupations in the Workforce: Sales workers represent 8.8 percent of the national workforce
- Median Annual Wage for sales as of May 2023: $36,760.00

There is motivation to push ourselves, to get a leg up that so many didn't have in their childhood. Because most of us come to sales by an indirect route, we are self-made, ambitious, driven, and up to the challenge that a routinely variable compensation model brings. We are risk-takers (not getting paid unless you make a sale tends to support this trait) and enjoy the opportunity to prove ourselves and reinvent ourselves weekly, quarterly, annually. We are change agents. Early adopters. We are highly responsive and move at a fast pace.

Some other traits of sales professionals, as revealed by personality tests, may surprise you. Many defy our typical stereotypes. Such traits include: modesty, conscientiousness, curiosity, being achievement-oriented, being upbeat, and perhaps most surprising, not being typically gregarious.[3]

Why did I choose sales? It was supposed to be a stop on the road, and instead it became my home. It wasn't the money. I was motivated by people and the connections. Putting the right people together to solve problems, do deals, get jobs, find board seats … it was all an opportunity for impact and to make a difference. I won't deny that there's a deep gratification and serious dopamine hit that comes from sales. Karl Marx espoused that the downfall of capitalism would be due to the alienation of the worker from the fruits of their labor. Sales is the antithesis of that. Closing deals and winning work can be a rush of immediate gratification. The sales professional is deeply connected and measured by their results and is able to point to them and say, "I did that!" It's a rewarding rush—emotionally, financially, and spiritually.

To quote one of my favorite authors and one of the best books on sales ever written, *To Sell Is Human* by Dan Pink, "Like it or not, we're all in sales now." Then why is it the case that as sales professionals we can feel so less than and allow the world at large to support that thinking? For my own journey, I found myself overcompensating for never really being treated like a "professional"—and at times

---

[3] Steve W. Martin. "Seven Personality Traits of Top Salespeople." *Harvard Business Review.* June 27, 2011. https://hbr.org/2011/06/the-seven-personality-traits-o

feeling like it was something for which I had to apologize. When I think of what that word means, "professional," the definition 100% includes sales professionals. A professional is:

A person who performs a job or task with a high level of competence and skill, especially one who adheres to a specific code of conduct and ethical standards.
—*Merriam-Webster Dictionary*

I experienced all these characteristics both personally as well as with my colleagues and team members. I was enamored with the creative and strategic thinking required to be successful at sales. From identifying which technology and enablement tools were ideal to support revenue growth, to how best to scope and penetrate key target accounts, to creating sales methodologies, the more I learned, the more I wanted to keep learning. Sales is complex, challenging, and vast, and is multi-faceted, depending on a range of factors. It's also the engine that drives revenue, and it's the backbone of what helped build our country. Sales professionals are inherently entrepreneurs and reflect the greater entrepreneurial spirit of the U.S. We are adaptable, quick on our feet, and able to pivot and change strategies as needed—all characteristics that reflect some of our best cultural qualities as a nation.

Instead of spending the first part of my career apologizing and embarrassed for being in sales, if I'd truly owned it, I wonder how much of my subsequent over____ (fill in the blank: drinking, eating, networking, etc.) would have been different.

The Sales Buddha's Corner
The Deal Beneath the Deal

When we think of how much of our energy goes into what other people think of us and their perceptions of what we do for a living, what car we drive, how big our house is … it can be exhausting. There's a phrase I've used many times with teams that I've managed that sums up how most of us are motivated: We are motivated by the need to look good or the fear of looking bad. Which are you? I'm both, thank you very much. Doesn't mean that I don't work on it daily, but both motivations will invariably creep up into my interactions. The opportunity is for us to notice it when it happens and give ourselves grace and self-compassion for being human.

What does this have to do with sales? The healthier we are physically and emotionally as sales professionals means that we bring that self-awareness and health to our clients, prospects, friends, and family, hence elevating the sales "brand." One of my podcast mentors, Michael Gervais, has a recent book entitled *The First Rule of Mastery: Stop Worrying about What People Think of You.* His concept of "FOPO: Fear of People's Opinions," calls out how our prioritization of others' opinions over our own values and aspirations limits our ability to be authentic. Because sales professionals can often come from a less than "pedigreed" background, we can often feel as if we are not enough or less than. Hence, we feel like we always must make up for something. This can drive us to accomplish great things but can simultaneously be soul-sucking. It can lead to overspending, overeating, overdrinking, and the excess that can make our profession a grind with high turnover and burnout. I would challenge all those within our profession to lean into the most authentic versions of ourselves possible and consider giving way fewer fucks about what others think.

3

Health Begins at Home

Once I got a taste of better health and what it was like to *feel* better, *look* better, *sleep* better, and *perform* better … it was game on. In my mind, if a little is good, more is better. As you can see from photos of me, I underwent an evolution, and it didn't happen overnight. TRUE wellness took time, research, dedication, and several guides along the way in the form of functional medicine doctors, longevity clinics, and personal trainers. I'll share the roadmap of my journey that gives a sense of the timeline, the progress, many detours, wins and failures, and current state.

It took me about six months to drop the forty pounds that I had gained over my first six years in sales. Once I started counting calories and working out three days a week, I had a protocol and I stuck to it. Unfortunately, because I was calorie-counting, the content of what I was eating was far from ideal. A splurge day would mean that all of my calorie allotment for that day could be used for a piece of cake, and then I'd have to fast the remainder of the day. Similarly, with alcohol, I would build in 300-400 calories a day for wine. Really, you ask? Really. As a result, even though I was nearly the ideal weight for my height, I was hardly at my best. Internally, I was inflamed, struggled with brain fog, and my energy levels were horribly inconsistent. So, the hard work at the gym and the discipline in food choices were definitely an improvement, but I still had work to do.

Wake Up Call

One day, I was at lunch with a good friend, and he mentioned his experience working with a functional medicine doctor (FMD) and the great health results that he was experiencing. I hadn't heard of "functional medicine" and only knew of the good old "regular" kind of doctors. A functional medicine doctor is a healthcare provider, often with specialized training, who takes a holistic approach to diagnose and treat chronic illnesses by addressing the underlying causes, rather than just the symptoms, through personalized plans that consider the whole person. Functional medical practitioners focus on the interconnectedness of the body's systems and how they influence each other rather than treating isolated symptoms. What a concept! My friend told me his doctor had run tests that at the time seemed unusual—hair tests, stool samples, and blood work—to look for various health markers, mycotoxins (mold), and heavy metals in the body. I was beyond intrigued! With a traditional MD, routine lab work is barely a sliver of insight into what is

> We each have our own bio-diversity, and it's essential to find what works best for us on an individual level.

really going on with us, and the reference ranges that they include for our results *are compared against the mass population instead of what is ideal for us as individuals.* I signed up with his doctor the same week. Looking back, I won't say that this guy was ideal, but I learned a ton, and it was my first experience getting laboratory blood work done and really understanding how to read my own results and have some agency over my health. We each have our own biodiversity, and it's essential to find what works best for us on an individual level.

That doctor also put me on the journey of understanding how critical the quality of what we consume is to our health. I learned to read ingredient labels and cut through the gunk to understand what I was really eating. Eventually, I put apps on my phone that would allow me to identify not only everything that was in the product I was thinking about consuming, but who that particular product's parent company was to better understand the supply chain of where it came from. He encouraged me to experiment with low-carb, carnivore, keto, and paleo diets to find which ones resonated with my body the best.

After looking at my blood work results, it was obvious that I was not well. He had run an exhaustive panel. My liver markers were up (hello, alcohol!), my hair analysis came back showing high levels of lead and cadmium, my hormone levels were off, and my "bad" cholesterol was far too high. He had also looked at my DNA and told me that I am a slow methylator, which means that I don't get toxins out of my body as fast as someone else who might have different DNA.

In my mind, I was eating well and exercising. Should my bloodwork results have been *that* bad? Looking back on it, I'm not surprised at those results, but at the time it absolutely scared me straight into action. It's one thing to enjoy sugar and alcohol occasionally, but when I saw my results on paper, there was zero denying my reality.

Food Inventory

The first thing my new FMD advised was for me to go through my home and do an inventory of food, personal and household products, and the house itself. It was critical that I understood what I was surrounding myself with every day that could be harmful and adding to the buildup of toxins in my body. I started with food, and I read labels on anything that came in a jar or bottle. I went through the refrigerator and the pantry to look for ingredients like "natural flavors," gluten, MSG, maltodextrin, bad seed oils like canola, sunflower, corn, and soybean, and toxic emulsifiers and thickeners like carrageenan, guar, and xanthan gums. It was eye-popping how many toxic ingredients were hidden in products that claimed to be "organic" or "healthy." Hardly! When I took a hard look at the meat that I was eating, little of it was grass-fed or pasture-raised. I, like so many people, had thought that saving money on great deals at the grocery store on commercial meat was a good thing—not realizing, of course, that commercially "farmed" chicken, beef, and pork all come from animals eating grain and soy that's covered in the world's favorite gut-destroying pesticide, glyphosate. I had been consuming these daily along with pesticide-covered vegetables with no idea how incredibly harmful they were to my gut and my microbiome.

Health really does all start "in the gut," as the saying goes. The microbiome in humans is often used to describe the microorganisms that live in or on a particular part of the body, such as the skin or gastrointestinal tract. These groups of microorganisms are dynamic and change in response to a host of environmental factors, such as exercise, diet, medication, and other exposures. The microbiome has many effects on our health, including digestion, immune system development, and vitamin synthesis. A healthy microbiome can reduce the risk of obesity, heart disease, diabetes, and cancer. It can affect how we respond to environmental substances, play a role in food allergies, kidney stones, Alzheimer's disease, Crohn's disease, colon cancer, and asthma. An imbalance of the microbiome, what is called dysbiosis, can lead to a whole host of health problems. Symptoms of dysbiosis include constipation, diarrhea, bloating, fatigue, brain fog, weight gain, and acid reflux.

Based on the food I was eating every day, I was putting myself right in the line of bad microbiome fire. The signs were all there in my health, performance, and cognition. I just never connected them together. Like other people, I recognized the value of "organic" when it came to buying food and meat that was preferably raised without pesticides or hormones, so I would occasionally splurge and buy organic. After working with our doctor, organic and "non-GMO" became a non-negotiable, as did buying meat that was grass-fed and pasture-raised. "You are what you ate, ate" as the saying goes. I realize that it's not always possible to buy organic, but it all builds up in us over time to absolutely affect how we feel, and it has a cumulative impact on our gut, microbiome, cognitive function, and energy levels. With vegetables, it's very similar. Ensure you're buying organic (and locally farmed!) veggies that aren't covered in pesticides as often as possible. We live in a world where the toxic burdens run high, so it's not about perfection. The key is to just do your best and have a strategy to keep toxics to the minimum that you can. If you love your favorite popcorn brand—keep it. Just try to offset it by swapping out something else with a cleaner version.

Water Review

Next, I moved on to investigate my water—both bottled water and tap water. I quickly recognized that it was far from ideal. I live in California, which is known for having high concentrations of arsenic in its water, and the filtration systems that arc used by cities only remove certain impurities. So, what you're drinking from the tap and bathing in likely contains microplastics, pesticides, nitrates, heavy metals, and leftover pharmaceuticals your neighbors are taking. Not kidding. And any water you're buying that's in plastic is loaded with microplastics in direct proportion to how long that water has been sitting in its container. Ewww!

It cost me about forty dollars to change out each of the showerheads to ones that filter out 98% of pollutants—worth it! I looked at various reverse osmosis systems that were reasonably priced so that my drinking water was optimized. Berkey and Aquatru both make great ones. What a difference clean water makes. From skin and energy to regular elimination (ahem!), the impact of clean water is everything.

Household Environment

After examining my food and water resources, I audited all of the personal and household products in my home. I had no idea that what we put *onto* our bodies can be almost as disruptive as what we put *into* them. I learned that topicals like shampoo, lotion, aftershave, toothpaste, nail polish, and cologne can contain ingredients that significantly disrupt the endocrine system and our hormones. Is it any wonder then why the testosterone levels in men have been in a steady decline for decades and why women are having more difficulty than ever getting pregnant. Or why low thyroid is so common? Many of the perfumes and makeup products that I was using contained known cancer-causing agents like talc and toxic dyes.

We live in a world where the toxic burdens run high, so it's not about perfection. The key is to just do your best and have a strategy.

After I said a sad (and expensive!) goodbye to all of my favorite scents, topicals, and smell goods, I never felt better. Strange headaches or slight congestion that I used to get after spraying my favorite perfume suddenly went away.

The household cleaners were equally as bad. It's amazing the bottles that we forget about under our sinks just sit there stealthily and quietly off-gassing horrible toxins. Things like insect sprays, abrasive cleaners, drain cleansers, bleach, paint … all contribute to quite the science project! In small doses or exposures, these products can serve a purpose, but keeping them around us daily is far from ideal for maintaining optimum health. I found it was far less expensive to buy organic or "clean" products from the store than the name-brand toxic ones that I was accustomed to. There are also great alternatives to almost all products that are better for your home and your family rather than reaching for the products we reference by their brand names. Once I removed these products from the house, I was shocked by what a difference it made.

We live in an economy where there will always be exposures to toxins, but the key is to minimize where you can and offset with a routine detoxing protocol. I heard one of my biohacking mentors once say that, "We are all born with a toxin bucket with a hole in the bottom. For some of us, the hole in the bottom of our toxic bucket is bigger than it is for others." If we don't take steps to manage it, once we get into our forties and fifties the wheels start falling off the bus and we wonder why. "Oh, it just happens when you get older—it's part of aging." No. It's not. The brain fog, joint pain, fatigue, and hormone dysregulation—to name a few—can absolutely be avoided if we take care to drain our toxic bucket regularly—and take measures to keep it from filling up too far in the first place.

House Audit

I had no idea how mold and heavy metals can disrupt so many of our biological systems and cause significant inflammation in our bodies. Exposure is often expressed through indicators like eczema breakouts, skin rashes, joint pain, respiratory issues, cognitive challenges, and migraines. These can all be signs that your toxic bucket is filling up.

With these kinds of environmental exposures in mind, I went through the physical surroundings of my house. I hadn't really thought about things like mold potentially being in my home or the impacts of the extermination company spraying chemicals around my house and yard every month. Nor had I thought about my house, which was built in 1903, being covered in lead paint. Paint that would chip. And fall onto furniture. And onto my floors. Where the dogs were. You get the picture. Ugh. So, with a $5 DIY kit from Amazon, I got busy swiping.

I did a full house audit and checked anywhere there might have been leaks or standing water due to poor run off, and looked behind panels for mold. I used the swabs to check for lead on dishware, glassware, and utensils. I replaced plastic utensils for wood or silicone options. I eliminated all non-stick cookware in favor of steel or cast-iron options, and changed out aluminum foil and plastic baggies for safer, glass containers. "Lead crystal" is exactly that: loaded with lead. And I had no idea that colored ceramics and anything that has lettering stenciled on the outside can be the highest in lead content. Many of my wine glasses didn't make the cut.

As for the pesticides, I looked for cleaner alternatives to keep the critters at bay. I switched to things like orange oil, white wine vinegar, lavender, cayenne, and lemon. I also took a hard look at the hot tub and pool. Chlorine can be toxic for humans.

Unsurprisingly, after six months, I retested and my levels had come down *significantly* in all categories. This was in huge part because I replaced bad food with better options, cleaned up my skin and hair regimens, and improved my home environment. All of this in addition to a great supplement protocol to assist with toxin elimination had me on a much better track.

Lab Work

Once you dive into the world of functional medicine, you realize that it is truly a world you've never entered before. To avoid going down rabbit holes and testing for many things that sound really cool but have no relevance nor insight, it's important to start your journey with someone who knows what to ask you and what to listen for. Different tests look for different things, and you need to understand what you're solving for. For example, I'd had a consistent rash on my left hand, and it also sometimes showed up under my nose in small patches. This was a new thing and certainly wasn't normal.

After speaking with my FMD, he shared that a lot of the time skin rashes and breakouts are related to mold. He asked me a series of questions about my environment that was extremely helpful and helped me to figure it out. "Are you eating berries that have mold on them? When you look closely at your shower tile, do you see any signs of mold? Are you buying cheap coffee or slightly more expensive that's single origin and organic? Is your air conditioning unit too powerful for the square footage of your home? Do you eat a lot of peanuts?" You get the idea. These things are very typical ways that people get mold exposure without knowing it.

Again, these kinds of substances all build up in our bodies over time. Sure enough, when we had purchased our 1903 San Francisco home, we had noticed mold under the stairs in the garage. We'd asked our contractor to fix it, and we trusted that he had. But by "fixing it" he meant painting over it. Not realizing the harmful effects of mold and thinking the issue was fixed, a few months later we used that fifty-square-foot area to create a home gym where we spent five days a week breathing heavy while we worked out. Still waiting for my IQ Award for that. Thank heavens my FMD was thoughtful and exhaustive in his questioning. Finally, this resulted in me saying goodbye to my rashes.

Supplements

Before sharing information on supplements, let me say that supplements should be just that—supplemental. They should augment, not replace. They should be used in a targeted way to offset what might be missing for a period, and should not be relied upon forever. Ideally, we should all be able to get one hundred percent of our nutrients directly from the food that we eat. Unfortunately, due to industrialized agriculture, the soil today isn't what it was 100 years ago. So, there are times when we are eating all the right foods, but they don't contain the nutrition or vitamins and minerals that they once did. This means that when we get lab work done, we need to pay attention to our micronutrient results to ensure that we are covering our bases. Micronutrients are critical to the body's ability to function on a myriad of levels. As they relate to supplements, they can be an important ally in our health and wellness journeys.

For me, it was important to augment my diet with specific supplements based on the diet protocol that was working best for me. Layered onto that was the need for supplements to assist with detoxification of the mold found on my mycotoxin report and the lead and cadmium found in my bloodwork and hair mineral analysis test. I used an app on my phone to track my food intake, which would subsequently show me not only what macronutrients I was taking in but also what micronutrients I was consuming or missing. With each of our respective dietary choices we are bound to miss some micronutrients occasionally. However, it's important to know if you're missing a particular vitamin or mineral *routinely*, especially if you're opting for a particular dietary protocol. If you're vegan, for example, you can miss B vitamins because many of the foods that contain them aren't consumed on that diet. If you're a carnivore, you need to make sure you're getting enough fiber and vitamin C, and so on. If you know that you're most likely exposed to toxins regularly because you live by a freeway or your neighbor is doing construction on their house, it's important to take gentle daily detoxifying things like garlic, cilantro, pectasol, spirulina, bentonite clay, etc. Because my hair mineral analysis and blood came back high with lead and cadmium, I took a specific protocol for heavy metals which combined Zeolite, EDTA, and charcoal. This supplement and detox protocol literally changed my life. I'll spend a lot of time on supplements in later chapters, because it's important for you to examine and figure out what's ideal for you and your own unique biodiversity.

> There are times when we are eating all the right foods, but they don't contain the nutrition or vitamins and minerals that they once did.

The Sales Athlete's Gym Bag
Steps You Can Take for a Cleaner, Healthier Lifestyle

How do you know if you should consider working with an FMD?

- Get with your regular MD or (better) a functional MD and tell them that you're really interested in optimizing your health. They should want to run labs to get a baseline of where your current health is and how your biomarkers and inflammatory markers are tracking.
- Note: As mentioned earlier, traditional MD ranges for most labs will be far laxer than a functional MDs, because they're comparing to the ranges for the rest of Americans who are eating the Standard American Diet (SAD).
- Most FMDs are willing to meet virtually.

What tests should you run?

- Talk to a licensed practitioner to give you a diagnostic of what your labs results really mean. Once you've done that, they'll have suggestions as to what makes the most sense, what might be covered by your insurance, etc.
- Should you not have access to a doctor or you're willing to take a stab at really digging into your own health, there are amazing websites and resources that are designed to be economical, but mostly out of pocket. Here are a few that provide you all sorts of lab testing options at reasonable prices that allow you to look more closely at your own health:

- * Everlywell
- * Rupa Health
- * Functional Health
- * SiPhox Health
- DNA testing is not just for finding long-lost relatives. It can be incredibly insightful as it relates to ascertaining your specific genetic markers, your epigenetics, how your body processes certain foods, fat, carbohydrate, caffeine, alcohol, and what might be ideal for you.

What diet is best for you?

- This is a big decision and one that should really be dialed in based on your discussions with a licensed nutritionist and/or MD, FMD. I do think that none of us can go wrong by focusing on eating whole foods that we know are healthy and nourishing.

Learn to read a food label.

- Ignore whatever claims are on the front of a package: "Natural, low-fat, fortified, multigrain, light, no added sugar, low calorie," etc.
- Product ingredients are listed by quantity—from highest to lowest—so scan the first three ingredients, as they make up the majority of what you'll be eating.
  - * If the first three ingredients are refined grains, a type of sugar, or hydrogenated oils, you can assume it's not healthy.
  - * The longer the ingredient list, the more processed the product is.

- * Pay attention to the "serving size" indicated. They are frequently smaller than what people will typically consume.
- Look out for hidden sugars.
  - * These include maltose, glucose, high-fructose corn syrup, disaccharides, fruit juice concentrate, dextran, and crystalline fructose, to name a few.

Audit yourself and your home.

- Can you change everything you use? That would be costly and unlikely, but do what's realistic for you. These phone apps are free, and you can use them to check your house, personal care, and food products for how "clean" they are before you make purchasing decisions:
  - * Think Dirty
  - * Yuka
  - * EWG
  - * Bobby Approved
- Consider changing your cookware from non-stick (Teflon is evil!) to stainless steel or cast-iron.
- EMFs! Our internet, electronic devices, and cell phones all put off electromagnetic radiation. Try to turn your phone off completely each night when you go to bed, or at least don't sleep with it next to your head.

Find Clean Food.

- Consider Thrive Market for amazing clean, organic, and healthy options based on your individual dietary protocol. It's delivered to your door!

- Consider the following regenerative farms for meat and seafood that allow you to order in bulk for a great price, are non-GMO, pasture raised, grass fed meat that deliver to your door. And bonus: You're supporting local farmers!
  * Family Friendly Farms
  * U.S. Wellness Meats
  * Frankie's Free-Range Meat
  * Seatopia
  * White Oak Pastures
  * Force of Nature
  * Apsey Farms
  * Wild Pastures
  * Primal Pasture
  * Butcher Box

The Sales Buddha's Corner
The Infinite Game

The Buddha taught, "To understand everything is to forgive everything." Maybe the future of sales, fitness, and mindfulness is about forgiveness of the hustle, the ego, the illusion that we have to earn worth through exhaustion or accomplishment.

When you train like an athlete, meditate like a monk, and travel like a minimalist, you start to live in alignment. You sell from coherence, not compensation. You win deals without losing yourself. That is the real championship.

The Executive/Sales Athlete of tomorrow won't chase success; she'll embody it. Her technology will be an ally, her health metrics a mirror, her presence a superpower.

The future isn't "more," it's targeted. It belongs to those who train their biology, their mind, and their mission to move as one. Sales is a sport—and this is how you play it for life.

4

Hacking the Room

've been accused of having *a lot* of energy. Those accusers are not wrong. (I can hear former colleagues chuckling from here). Not frantic or scattered energy … just a lot. Some of the best coaching I ever received from a mentor was, "Nicole, you would benefit from a stronger awareness of the impact your energy can have on the dynamics of a room." It was an eye opener for me. Going forward, I learned to appreciate the dynamics and interplay between energies in a sales context. It wasn't about my energy not being "okay," it was about being mindful of it and the energy of others. The more we attune ourselves to the dynamics every client or prospect meeting holds, the more successful outcomes we get. It's about syncing our physiology so completely that our steadiness becomes a tuning fork for the vibe of the room. Every room has a nervous system, and the best performers don't just walk into it—we help regulate it. We hack it.

The Physiology of Presence

Presence begins in the body, not the brain. Neuroscientist Andrew Huberman explains that the autonomic nervous system—the partnership of the sympathetic "go" and parasympathetic "slow"—decides whether you enter a room as threat or safety. When your breathing is shallow, your shoulders are forward, or you're distracted, you broadcast stress signals before you speak. Maintaining high heart rate variability (HRV), balanced breath, and steady eye contact communicates confidence at a primal level. In sales, our job is to sense the micro-shifts in posture, tone, or silence that reveal engagement or resistance. We can't do that well if we aren't aware of our own.

Before your meeting starts, drop in to where your feet are and get grounded. Dropping your shoulders down and back, while you take three deep breaths tells your vagus nerve that you're "safe." True influence is equal parts command and connection. Physiologically, this balance mirrors sympathetic and parasympathetic activation—assertive energy met with grounded calm. We often think that presence equals charisma; but in reality, it's coherence—the synchronization between our heart rhythm, breath, and brain waves. Biofeedback studies show that when one person achieves coherence, nearby people subconsciously mirror that rhythm. Real hacks to achieve this include slowing your pace of speech and slightly lowering your voice. It's not about being overly performative. It's about conducting.

Hacking the Environment

We can't always choose the room, but we can hack its variables. Things like natural lighting, temperature, and food/drinks all play an important role and speak to our biology. Natural lighting boosts alertness. Fluorescents do the opposite: They crush dopamine. Even when you're the guest, you can ask for the blinds to be opened. Where you sit also sends a message. I've preached this for years in sales, but in a prospect or client meeting always, *always* take the "bad seat." Do you think anyone likes the seat with their back to the door? Um, no. By taking that seat, you're automatically starting off your meeting by putting your clients, prospects, or important guests more at ease. Recognize the temperature in the room is also important. Studies from the *Journal of Environmental Psychology* show that cooler rooms (around 68–70 °F) result in maintaining attention longer. A warm room breeds lethargy. Lastly—and maybe most importantly—for meetings that have food involved, opt for fruit, yogurt, salad options vs. the box of donuts, muffins, or sandwiches.

> Presence begins in the body, not the brain.

Micro-Recovery Between Meetings

Meetings can stack like interval sprints. Without allowing ourselves time for recovery and the opportunity to "reset," we are limiting our ability to fully show up for our clients and prospects. If we don't give ourselves the opportunity to shake off the prior meeting or phone call, we are potentially carrying that energy with us and projecting it onto the next one. Between meetings, allow yourself to step outside and get some daylight and fresh air. This not only helps reset your circadian rhythm but gives you a gentle dopamine boost. Take a moment to hydrate with some minerals or electrolytes. If there aren't any handy, put a pinch of salt and a squeeze of lemon into your water. Give yourself three minutes to just breathe. Box-breathing is ideal: Four in, four hold, four out, four hold. And repeat. Reframe your thinking for the upcoming meeting and ask yourself, "What's my intention heading into the next meeting? What's my desired outcome?" These things will help you reground and balance yourself coherently for a fresh start. It's often said that it's not how much we fail, but how fast we can recover. Your ability to reset quickly is what separates sales professionals from top performers.

The Sales Athlete's Toolkit

- **Red-light panel or clip-on lamp:** Boost mitochondria and mood when you don't have access to windows.
- **Noise-canceling earbuds:** Create your own pre-game silence ritual. Or play binaural beats for relaxed alertness and presence at 8-12Hz.
- **Sensate 2 device:** Try using a vibrational vagal stimulation before presentations.
- **Hydration protocol:** Start the day with electrolytes; end with magnesium.
- **Sleep hygiene:** Keep the same bedtime, even on road weeks. Circadian consistency fuels authority.

Story from the Floor
Read the Room

The meeting started like the other quarterly reviews we'd had with the CFO and CLO of a large public company client—sleek conference room, decks prepped, coffees in hand. But something was off. The client team, normally warm and engaged, were sitting back in their chairs, displaying low energy and appearing distracted. Most sales professionals would have plowed through the agenda, pretending not to notice. But the Sales Athlete in me felt it immediately—that subtle dissonance in the air, the collective exhale that didn't land. So, I paused. Closed my laptop. "Can we pause for a moment?" I asked gently. "I might be wrong, but something feels different today. Is something going on behind the scenes that we should address before we start diving into what we've prepared?"

The room went quiet. The CFO sighed. Turns out, a restructuring announcement had gone out that morning. Half the leadership team was uncertain about their roles. They didn't need a proposal. They needed a conversation.

We dropped the slides and started talking about what was changing in their risk landscape and how they were going to navigate the uncertainty. We were able to listen and better understand how our respective networks and connections in the market might be helpful to them. We shared industry insights to assist them with market perspective. By the end of the meeting, the energy had changed completely—from guarded to grounded. The takeaway? Great sales professionals "pitch." Sales Athletes "attune."

If you're rested, recovered, and regulated, every situation is an opportunity for you to add value and contribute to the dynamic in a game changing way. Ensuring that your head and heart are 100% where your feet are is the greatest competitive advantage you can have.

The Sales Buddha's Corner
The Room Is a Mirror

Ancient teachers called it wu wei—effortless action. Modern neuroscience calls it flow state. Different languages, same truth: Alignment creates results. When you walk into a boardroom, a dinner, or a negotiation, imagine every heart in that room beating in rhythm with yours. The goal isn't dominance; it's coherence. Your inner calm becomes the tuning fork that brings chaos back into harmony. Before every meeting, every pitch, every moment that matters, ask, "Who do I need to be for this room to remember its potential?" And then breathe that answer into existence.

5

Navigating Hacks
The Road Warrior's Guide to Peak Performance on the Move

love airports. And why not? I spend a lot of time in them. I've hacked them. I've dialed in where I can get the cleanest bites, the best lounge experience. I know where I can get my shoes shined and my nails touched up. There's a place at LAX—usually at the Terminal 1 security gate—when I can tell who travels for sport and who travels for survival. The pros—we move like swimmers slicing water: deliberate, calm, minimal drag. Everyone else is flapping. I used to be the flapper. Laptop half-charged, panicked to get to my gate, latte in one hand, inbox at DEFCON 4. Then I realized: For sales professionals, travel is sport. We can't outsource the miles. The only way to win is to lean in and train for the road the way an athlete trains for altitude.

Jet-Lag Math and Circadian Warfare

Our physiology doesn't care about frequent-flier status. Each 1,000 miles flown east steals roughly an hour of circadian rhythm. Dr. Satchin Panda calls light "the master switch" for the body clock. He recommends that two days before your flight, you shift bedtime by one hour toward your destination. Once in the air, do your best to put yourself on the time zone to which you're traveling and swap the alcohol for electrolytes. Once you're there, you're there. BE in that time zone. This will reset your circadian rhythm and melatonin faster than any pill could do. There's even some good research coming out now about "grounding" (putting your bare feet on local earth) once you arrive at your destination so that you can decrease jet lag and improve your recovery time.

When I recently arrived in Paris at dawn, I walked outside to stare at the horizon for a full two minutes. Yes, the doorman thought I was a nutter, but that light told my pituitary gland that I was in a new time zone now. It's the cheapest biohack in the book. Neuroscientist Andrew Huberman reminds us that light is the steering wheel for circadian rhythm. "Light early, darkness late."

Fueling on the Fly

Airports are metabolic minefields. Literally, they are carnivals of inflammation disguised as convenience. All of that pretty packaging is *designed* to pull us in. My rule: Eat for clarity, not for comfort. I make it a point to travel with clean snacks from home that give me some good options so I'm not nearly as tempted—things like Chomps Turkey Sticks, nuts, or a bag of carrots and cauliflower. I also bring my own organic tea and organic coffee powder so I'm not drinking whatever the brown water is that they serve on the plane. On an LAX to JFK flight, I once skipped the airline "omelet" (which literally had the visible texture of an old business plan) and pulled out my travel kit: a small shaker of greens, a packet of collagen, and almonds I'd weighed out at home. The guy next to me looked at me like I was prepping for surgery. I landed sharper than he did and didn't need a triple espresso to fake energy at my important client meeting that afternoon.

Other things I always bring are protein powder, creatine, and magnesium. Hydrating is huge, as we need one liter of water per five hours that we are airborne. And just say "no" to caffeine after 2 p.m. local time, because sleep is the currency of resilience, and caffeine will not help your hydration levels or your ability to get some shut eye. When you know you have a long flight, do your best to prepare in advance. It's usually why I splurge for business class—so that I can get good sleep and land awake, refreshed and adjusted to the local time zone. My ritual: comfortable clothing, compression socks (they're a thing!), and noise-canceling headphones playing low-hertz binaural beats. Before takeoff, two minutes of slow exhale breathing. HRV up, mind down. I track my sleep like revenue. A single bad night compounds reaction time by 20 percent—roughly the cognitive drop of being tipsy. That's not who you want leading your pitch in Frankfurt.

Fueling principles:
- Protein first. Shoot for 30g per meal. This stabilizes glucose and mood.
- Pack smart snacks like almonds, jerky, 85 percent dark chocolate.
- Hydration ratio: 1 liter of water per 5 hours of flight time. Add trace minerals or electrolytes.
- One glass of wine in the air equals three glasses on land.

Jet Lag Correction:
- Spend fifteen minutes in sunlight before drinking coffee.
- Use creatine to support cognitive clarity and cellular hydration.

Ben Greenfield says, "Travel doesn't ruin your biology. Your choices do."

Hotel hacks

I've become completely comfortable asking hotel staff what would seem to a nearby listener as very strange questions.

"What's the darkest and quietest room in this hotel?"

"If you were a vampire, which room would you pick for yourself?"

"Are there any children staying in any of the rooms near the one that you've assigned me?" (Sorry kids!)

My goal isn't to shock. It's making sure that I can truly get a fantastic night of sleep and be one hundred percent ready for the next day. Once I'm in my coffin—I mean room—I go to work. I unplug the alarm clocks and anything else that has little glowing blinkie lights, drop the room temperature to 67 degrees, plug a towel under the door to block hallway light, and pull out my earplugs and eye mask. Bonus points if you remember your lavender scented essential oil to help waft you into dreamland. When I wake up, instead of using the moldy coffee machine my room offers, I bring my own instant mushroom coffee powder and a small, travel size hot water boiler. It's easy to pack, and I can use it for both coffee in the morning and tea before bedtime. I also travel with packets of monk fruit or stevia and powdered collagen creamer to avoid the necessity of using whatever the hotel might have to offer. And rather than paying $7.50 a bottle for the Fiji water in your room, the hotel gym usually has filtered water that I happily poach.

Movement Matters

I'm a big believer in keeping my workouts going while I travel. It makes a significant difference in your resilience from travel and how you mentally show up to your important meetings. If your hotel has a gym, then it's a no-brainer. If not, I travel with resistance bands. They are a terrific hack that take up very little luggage space and are inexpensive. They will give you a terrific workout right in your hotel room, as they combine both concentric and eccentric movements. I also have several apps on my phone with great workouts at the ready including HIIT (high intensity interval training) and using body weight that are great for sneaking a quick workout in while in my hotel room. It's also important to keep your steps up while you are traveling. It gives you the excuse to get "off the beaten path" and go explore the city in which you are staying. That said, last year while in London, I chose to avoid the monsoon outside and instead paced my hotel room to hit my step count for the day while watching a great film.

If we have the will—there's usually a way. Travel is now like a meditation in motion. And when delays inevitably hit, I hear Peter Crone's voice: "How is this happening *for* you?" So I use the downtime for reflection—HRV breathing, journaling, or stretching while everyone else doomscrolls. My Oura ring calls it recovery. I call it sovereignty. Every time you choose coherence over chaos, you reclaim power that most people hand to circumstance.

Toolkit for the Traveling Sales Athlete

- **Noise-canceling headphones:** Create a sanctuary anywhere.
- **Electrolyte packets:** Jet Fuel Lite or LMNT
- **Sensate 2 or Apollo Neuro:** Vagus nerve calm on command
- **Foldable or travel size red-light panel:** Morning mitochondria, evening wind-down
- **Compression boots:** Because your calves shouldn't hate you for success

The Sales Buddha's Corner
Stillness at 35,000 Feet

Somewhere between takeoff and landing, you realize: Travel is just a metaphor for consciousness. The body moves; awareness stays. At altitude, the plane hums, the seatbelt sign blinks, and time feels suspended. That's presence in its rawest form—nothing to fix, nowhere to go. If you choose it, your flight time can be a rare opportunity for some peace and solitude. It's an opportunity to drop into your breath and rejuvenate. When I close my eyes mid-flight, I picture every client, every colleague, every future meeting aligned like stars on a route map—each one a chance to bring steadiness to turbulence. Stillness isn't the absence of motion. It's mastery within motion. So, the next time you're chasing platinum status at 35,000 feet, remember: your true upgrade is energetic. Breathe in coherence. Exhale control. Arrive as the calm that others tune into.

$$6$$

Wear Yourself Out
Hacking Feedback, Flow, and
the Future of Performance

I t started with a buzz, a tiny vibration mid-meeting that said, "You've been sitting too long." I was in the middle of an important prospect meeting, so I ignored it. Then the second buzz hit. Take a breath. That was my first week with the WHOOP strap—a health tracking wearable.

By Friday, it had taught me something that years of hard work, business acumen, and selling expertise never had: Self-awareness has a biometric signature. Today, we're all walking dashboards. Rings, bands, patches, neural sensors, glasses. Our bodies are producing data faster than our brains can process it. The question isn't whether to track; it's how to translate and get real meaning from all of that data.

> Self-awareness has a
> biometric signature.

From Guesswork to Feedback

At the heart of biohacking is the desire to tighten our feedback loops. The data from wearables, devices, lab work, etc. is all a way of getting at our own bio-individual needs. There was a time when performance lived in the land of "feel." "How'd you sleep?" "Pretty good, I think." Now, we have graphs for that. Wearables have turned the invisible visible—turning heart rate variability (HRV), sleep cycles, temperature, and strain into feedback loops. It's like having a pit crew in your pocket. When my Oura ring first told me my recovery was 31 percent, I wanted to argue, "no way!" Later that morning, when I came up short on a presentation I should have nailed, I realized that the truth hurts. Once we "know," we can't NOT know. The data wasn't judging me; it was informing me. The body keeps score, and wearables help us read that scorecard before it becomes burnout. They can give us incredible insights into what's happening on a deeper, physiological level.

The Biofeedback Revolution

The word biofeedback used to sound clinical. Now it's personal. Every device—from Apple Watch to WHOOP 5.0—acts as a mirror to your nervous system. The vagus nerve has become the new Wi-Fi connection between our minds and our bodies. It's like embodied analytics with your HRV telling you if your system is in flow or fight, while your resting heart rate whispers how well you're recovering. When executives learn to correlate data with story—"My sleep dropped because I had three glasses of cab after that client dinner"—they move from reactive to responsive. When knowing our own biofeedback bridges our physiology and our leadership abilities by linking our nervous-system regulation to decision quality and emotional intelligence, that's when biohacking becomes leadership.

The Science of Self-Regulation

Neuroscience has finally caught up to intuition. HRV is the scorecard of your nervous system—high means adaptable, low means reactive. In a world obsessed with acceleration, the real edge isn't speed; it's stability. Self-regulation is the modern executive's superpower: the ability to modulate your internal state so that your physiology supports your intention instead of sabotaging it. Neuroscience shows that the autonomic nervous system—the body's unconscious operating system—runs nearly every internal process related to focus, emotion, and performance. When you're under stress, the sympathetic branch takes over: heart rate spikes, cortisol floods, blood leaves the prefrontal cortex (the decision-making center). The result? You get tunnel vision, reactive thinking,

In a world obsessed with acceleration, the real edge isn't speed; it's stability. Self-regulation is the modern executive's superpower.

and impulsive communication. These erode precision, empathy, and judgment—the very qualities that make deals and lead teams. Dr. Andrew Huberman explains it like this: "Your state governs your story." When your physiology is balanced, your perception widens. When it's fried, every question feels like a threat. Wearables give you a second-by-second window into that system.

- Low HRV? Take five minutes of box breathing.
- Elevated resting heart rate? Hydrate and walk.
- Temperature spike or low recovery day? Delay that workout; your immune system is busy.

When we use these tools, they can become mirrors of mastery and help us identify patterns: the 4 p.m. crash after back-to-back Zooms, the improved coherence on mornings we meditate, the way our capacity for ideas expands when sleep is optimized. Awareness leads to agency, and you shift from reactive management to regulated leadership and performance.

Story from the Floor
The Night the Data Called Me Out

Last year in San Francisco, after a marathon day of meetings, I ignored every recovery cue. My Oura ring flashed red, WHOOP yelled, "Overreaching," and my phone suggested breathwork. I smiled, ordered another glass of wine, and stayed out until 2 a.m.

The next morning, I felt like a hungover blob. Cringing, with one eye open, I looked at my wearable scores. My resting heart rate had spiked, HRV was a flat line, and deep and REM sleep were in the single digit percentile. Ugh. I walked into my client meeting foggy and way beneath my best—until the COO, a triathlete, pointed to her wristband with a perky fresh smile and said, "HRV 78. What's yours?" With an ashamed grin, I showed her mine: 18. We laughed. Then she said something that stuck: "It's not about our velocity; it's about our direction. We all have the occasional night out; it's what we are choosing day after day that's moving us closer to our mountain or not." I realized that we all deserve grace now and then, but it's truly the steady drip that counts. Wearables and technology give us an accountability measure in our lives. Once we consciously know what gets us great results and what doesn't, it's much easier to make the good choices.

The Sales Athlete's Tech Stack

Every elite performer curates a stack:

- **Oura Ring:** recovery and readiness intelligence
- **WHOOP 5.0:** strain, HRV, sleep debt, and daily coaching
- **Sensate 2:** vagus nerve vibration for instant calm
- **Continuous Glucose Monitor (CGM):** real-time energy economics
- **Eight Sleep Pod:** thermal regulation = circadian consistency

Each tool gives a fragment of the truth. Combined, they create a digital nervous system—a feedback architecture for self-leadership.

From Data to Wisdom

One morning on a flight to Seattle, I was toggling between all of my dashboards—HRV, recovery, glucose—when a quiet thought surfaced. "If you keep tracking everything, when will you pause to actually be here now?" That line hit harder than jet lag. It reminded me that biohacking isn't about becoming robotic. It's about remembering we're human. Overtracking can turn awareness into anxiety, and I don't think we can live "optimized" 24/7 without losing the plot. I closed the app, stared out the window, and watched the clouds. For the first time that week, I wasn't optimizing. I was *being*. Ironically, my HRV jumped twenty points that day. Sometimes the most advanced technology is attention. If my Oura tells me I slept poorly, I can still choose to show up powerfully. The data is input, not identity.

There's a curve in personal growth: data, insight, integration, wisdom. Most people stop at data. They screenshot, post, and never change their behavior. Insight happens when our numbers meet the narrative. "I'm tired" becomes "My REM sleep dipped because I scrolled TikTok for an hour before bed." Integration is when our behavior shifts—when we stop bragging about all-nighters and start bragging about recovery scores. Wisdom is when we stop bragging altogether. We just embody. Wearables can't give you that final step—but they can light the path.

> Wisdom is when you stop bragging altogether. You just embody.

Story from the Floor
The Team That Hacked Flow

I was chatting with a fellow sales leader and biohacker, and she shared a great story with me about an initiative some of her team had launched. Her regional sales teams had invested in wearables for the entire group and started tracking sleep and HRV before and after every major prospect meeting. They did this for an entire quarter. At the end of the quarter, they each reported back and competed on their collective recovery scores against various metrics including their deal win/loss ratios. No surprise that the winning team reported back higher energy, better preparation, more creativity and insights brought to clients, better teamwork, increased close rate, and more revenue to the firm. The future of high performance is integrating data and recovery into strategy.

The Sales Buddha's Corner
The Inner Dashboard

There's a pulse deeper than your heart rate, a rhythm beyond REM cycles. It's the heartbeat of awareness itself. Ancient mystics didn't need wearables—they were the wearable. They felt their own coherence through breath, silence, intuition. Technology is simply catching up to what consciousness has always known: The body is data, and the soul is the analyst. So, when your ring glows red or your strap warns you to rest, that's your higher intelligence speaking in code. You can call it HRV. I call it harmony. The ultimate biohack is trust. Trust that your body is wise, your tech is a teacher, and your awareness is the interface between the two. Integrate, don't idolize. So wear yourself out— in the best way possible. Not from depletion, but from devotion. Not chasing numbers, but chasing nuance. And when the dashboard dims and the body quiets, listen for that steady rhythm underneath it all. Presence is, after all, the original wearable. That's you. Fully online. Fully alive.

7

Supplemental Hacks
Fuel, Focus & the Future of Enhancement

The cabinet that looked like a lab … it started innocently, with a bottle of magnesium. Then came the fish oil, vitamin D, adaptogens, mushroom tinctures, and a mysterious vial labeled BPC-157. One morning I opened my kitchen cabinet and realized it looked less like wellness and more like Walter White in an episode of *Breaking Bad*. But here's the thing. Unlike fads and powders promising "limitless____," my stack worked. The difference wasn't quantity; it was strategy. The modern sales athlete doesn't swallow everything on TikTok's Top 10 list. She curates like a bio-pharmacist: targeted, informed, purpose-driven.

> When your body is your instrument, the goal isn't more—it's mastery of your bio-individuality.

Because when your body is your instrument, the goal isn't more—it's mastery of your bio-individuality.

Cognition: The Thinking Edge

The best sales professionals who I know recognize that proposals and pretty PowerPoint slideshows don't win work. Sales isn't about scripts; it's about listening, curiosity, and asking great questions—all of which require a lot of brain power. The sharper your brain, the smoother your pitch. I only wish I had known in the earlier part of my career how much my choices to late night network, over-drink, and eat late were impacting my ability to show up at my best. I would say that my operating average was 70 percent of my total capacity. Such a shame when I think of how dialing in my nutrition, sleep, and supplementation would have allowed me to really excel and most importantly, contribute more to my colleagues and my teams.

"Nootropics" (from the Greek noos = "mind" and tropein = "to turn or bend") are substances that enhance cognitive performance, especially functions like focus, memory, motivation, and creativity, without causing dependency or significant side effects when used responsibly. They influence the brain in several ways:

- Increasing neurotransmitter activity (e.g., acetylcholine, dopamine, serotonin)
- Improving cerebral blood flow and oxygenation
- Enhancing neuroplasticity and the brain's ability to adapt and form new connections
- Optimizing mitochondrial energy production to improve mental endurance

Nootropics is a part of biohacking that dials in supplementation to support brain function optimization, and it's an area that has always interested me. Here are some examples.

Natural Compounds:
- Caffeine and L-theanine provide energy without the buzzy feeling.
- Rhodiola rosea for a pre-meeting and pre-workout lift
- Bacopa monnieri
- Mucuna pruriens: natural L-DOPA source—just respect the dose.
- Lion's Mane mushroom
- Cordyceps: altitude in a capsule; oxygen efficiency skyrockets.
- Ginkgo Biloba
- Probiotic strains like L. rhamnosus GG and B. longum. Happy microbiome, happy mind.
- Saffron extract: proven in meta-analyses to rival mild antidepressants for mood lift without side effects

Nutraceuticals/biohacker favorites:
- Alpha-GPC
- L-tyrosine: precursor to dopamine; sharpens motivation under stress
- Acetyl-L-carnitine
- Creatine

Clinical/synthetic nootropics (require a prescription):
- Modafinil
- Noopept, Piracetam, Aniracetam

For any high performer, nootropics can be seen as mental performance fuel to help maintain clarity, creativity, and focus while under pressure. But they're most effective when built on a foundation of sleep, nutrition, hydration, and recovery. They aren't a substitute for the basics—they *supplement* and *amplify* the basics.

Digestion: Trust Your Gut

Gut chaos is the hidden saboteur of performance. If digestion drags, energy flags, and your charisma dies by 2 p.m. Sometimes, no matter how hard we try to biohack our way through work travel, things can still misfire. About a year ago, after back-to-back road weeks fueled by airport salads, hotel food cooked in bad seed oils, and less than ideal sources of fiber, I got home and ran a stool test (welcome to adulting). My gut was off—dysbiosis city. After a week of psyllium husk, digestive enzymes, glutamine, and some good probiotics, everything was back to normal.

> Gut chaos is the hidden saboteur of performance.

The Core Four:
- **Digestive enzymes:** take with protein-heavy meals.
- **Bitters or apple cider vinegar:** kick-start gastric acid before eating.
- **Probiotics + prebiotics:** diversity = resilience. Rotate strains like you rotate workouts.
- **Glutamine + Zinc carnosine:** repair gut lining after travel food trauma.

The Frontier: Peptides & Bioregulators

Here's where things get sci-fi. Peptides are short amino-acid chains that act like cellular text messages that tell your cells what to do—precise, fast, and potent. Some increase collagen production. Others enhance fat metabolism, improve sleep, support muscle growth, or speed up recovery. Peptides are powerful because they mimic natural biological signals. They don't override systems like pharmaceuticals often do. They remind the body how to perform optimally again. I've been using peptides and bioregulators for about five years now. They are a game changer. Here are some examples of the most common ones.

Performance & Recovery:

- **BPC-157:** the "Body Protection Compound." Repairs tissue, gut lining, even tendons.
- **TB-500 (Thymosin Beta-4):** accelerates healing and reduces inflammation.
- **GHK-Cu (Copper peptide):** boosts collagen & skin repair; also cognitive benefits.

Longevity & Neuroprotection:

- **Epitalon/Epithalon:** telomere maintenance = younger cells
- **DSIP (Delta Sleep-Inducing Peptide):** deeper REM without dependency
- **Semax & Selank:** Russian-engineered cognitive peptides—focus, calm, creativity

Bioregulators:

Bioregulators are even smaller peptide fragments, usually two to four amino acids long, that act almost like genetic switches. They're derived from natural tissue extracts (such as thymus, pineal gland, liver, etc.) and work by turning on or off specific gene expression to restore function at the cellular level. Think software patch, not hardware hack. They were originally developed to help astronauts recover faster from stress, radiation, and aging while in space. Some examples of common ones are below:

- **Epitalon:** from the pineal gland; supports circadian rhythm and telomere length
- **Thymogen/Vladonix:** from thymus; supports immune system regulation
- **Cortexin:** brain bioregulators that enhance cognition and neuroprotection
- **Caralax:** supports connective tissue and vascular health

After tearing a rotator cuff snowboarding, I combined BPC-157 and GHK-CU injections with red-light therapy and collagen. My orthopedist was baffled at the speed of recovery. The data geek in me wasn't. Peptides close feedback loops that nature can leave open. I think peptides and bioregulators are one of the key components in the future of healthspan—meaning the portion of your life spent in vibrant, functioning health, as opposed to lifespan which is the total number of years you're alive.

Stack Wisdom: Your Stack is Your Superpower

Supplements aren't soloists; they're a symphony. The secret is stack design. I think this is true not only for supplementation but for us as human beings. Our unique stack of skills and experiences create us each to be one of a kind. Our unique "stack" can be our superpower … and our most competitive advantage. Whether it's your "life stack" or your supplementation stack, each reflects your own complex design and bio-individuality.

Morning Stack (activation):
- Hydration + electrolytes
- Adaptogen (Rhodiola or Cordyceps)
- Creatine
- B-complex + Magnesium Threonate
- Light + movement = dopamine ignition

Midday Stack (stabilization):
- Greens + collagen shake
- L-Theanine + Caffeine (if needed)
- Multiple vitamin
- Probiotic / Digestive enzymes with lunch

Evening Stack (regeneration):
- Magnesium Glycinate or Malate
- L-Glycine + Taurine for GABA support
- Zinc + Vitamin D with fat source
- Optional DSIP or Melatonin micro-dose

The Dark Side of Supplementation

Data without intuition becomes addiction. I've seen execs panic over a missed supplement like they missed payroll. The truth: more pills does not equal more power. There's a difference between having a rigid routine and having a system.

Systems are frameworks that adapt rather than collapse when conditions shift. Systems are rooted in principles, not perfection, and they're guided by feedback not formulas. Rigidity is ego-driven: It wants to control. Systems are awareness driven: They seek coherence. The Sales Athlete knows that the key is to build resilience that bends without snapping. If I forget my nootropics on a trip, I trust the fundamentals: breath, light, hydration, mindset. Supplements amplify—they don't replace—habits.

Why Functional Medicine Philosophy is Like Business

In business and in sales, you don't wait for a situation with a client to fail. You continually study performance metrics and ask deep questions. You stay in tune with changes and continually upgrade. Most people see a doctor *after* they get sick.

Functional medicine flips the script on this. You go to a functional medicine practitioner to understand why your system might become unwell and how to optimize it before symptoms appear. It's preventative. It's not "sick care." It's *performance care*. For example, traditional medicine often stops at diagnosis. "You have high cholesterol. Here's a statin." Functional medicine asks, "Why is your body making excess cholesterol in the first place?" and "Is it inflammation? Insulin resistance? Chronic stress? A nutrient deficiency?" Instead of patching the symptom, you're identifying the upstream imbalance, the metabolic or environmental trigger that started the cascade.

Functional labs typically go deeper than annual checkups. They give you a data map for your unique bio-individuality—which allows precision strategy rather than guesswork. What gets measured gets mastered. Functional medicine answers by testing, not guessing. I learned early on in my health journey that regular lab work, stool testing, hair mineral analysis, and DNA testing could provide incredible insights as to what was "going on under my hood."

Key labs worth running semi/annually:
- Micronutrient panel (SpectraCell/Genova)
- Comprehensive stool test
- Hormone + cortisol map
- Inflammation markers: hs-CRP, homocysteine
- Blood sugar metrics: fasting insulin & HbA1c

The Sales Buddha's Corner
The Alchemy of Enough

Here's the cosmic joke: After all the stacks, capsules, and quantified everything, the most potent supplement is self-trust. Ancient alchemists sought the philosopher's stone; modern biohackers chase mitochondrial bliss. Both are metaphors for transformation. The body is not a project to perfect—it's an ally to partner with. When you pop a capsule, do it with gratitude, not greed. When you inject a peptide, set intention, not expectation.

Because chemistry follows consciousness. So yes, build your stack. Test, iterate, refine. But also leave room for mystery, for the mornings when sunlight itself feels like NAD+, and laughter replaces L-Theanine. Fuel for focus, yes—but also for joy. That's the best upgrade protocol.

8

Hacking Your Way
Making the Most of the
Resources Available

The day I realized Google wasn't a doctor happened somewhere between my third search for "adrenal fatigue" and a $400 pile of supplements promising to "reset everything." I had the data, the wearables, the discipline—but no strategy. I wasn't healing; I was guesstimating. That's when I learned the secret every true biohacker eventually discovers: you can't DIY your physiology forever. We can listen to podcasts, follow experts, but at some point, you need a team that can help you glue it all together. And trust me ... I love an "easy button," but when it comes to our health and the "sickcare system," it's imperative that we take agency for our health

> The job isn't to find one perfect guru; it's to build an ecosystem of expertise that keeps you accountable, measured, and evolving.

and seek out the right expertise at the right time to guide us. Elite performers don't train alone. They have coaches, nutritionists, recovery specialists. Your biology deserves the same infrastructure. You're essentially the CEO of You, Inc. Your health team is your executive board. The job isn't to find one perfect guru; it's to build an ecosystem of expertise that keeps you accountable, measured, and evolving.

Where to Start: The Functional Medicine On-Ramp

As referenced in the last chapter, functional medicine flips the traditional model. Instead of "What disease do you have?" it asks, "Why did your system stop functioning optimally?" "Test, don't guess," says Dr. Stephen Cabral. "You can't change what you don't measure." Here are some entry points that actually work:

- **Function Health:** founded by Dr. Mark Hyman and Carly Kloss—150+ biomarkers, private dashboard, lifestyle tracking
- **IFM-certified practitioners (ifm.org/find-a-practitioner):** gold standard directory for functional and integrative physicians
- **Wild Health and Forward:** concierge clinics combining genomics, labs, and telecoaching
- **Everlywell, Rupa Health, Marek Diagnostics:** go from wondering to doing with at-home testing and virtual care.
- **The DNA Company and InsideTracker:** for personalized genetic and blood-biomarker optimization

Each of these resources is targeted in a way that allows you to go deeper in your understanding of what's really going on within your bio-individuality. When you order labs through these memberships and platforms, you empower yourself to look into the root causes of whatever symptoms you may have. That's what leads to real healing.

How to Read Your Own Labs (Without a PhD)

Most doctors will hand you a "normal" range. Functional medicine asks, "But is it optimal?" Here's a quick reference for common markers:

System	Functional Range	Why it Matters
Fasting Glucose	70-85 mg/dL	Above 90 = metabolic friction
hs-CRP	< 1 mg/L	Your inflammation barometer
Ferritin	50-100 ng/mL	Energy transport & thyroid synergy
Vitamin D	50-70 ng/mL	Immune & hormonal balance
Cortisol (AM)	10-18 Âµg/dL	Adrenal rhythm cue
HRV	60-100+	Nervous-system resilience index

About five years ago, after a particularly brutal Q4, my lab results screamed "inflammation." My functional MD noticed ferritin and CRP rising—classic over working, overtraining, over everything signals. We added omega-3s, dialed in my sleep hygiene, underwent three acupuncture treatments and an infrared sauna protocol. Within six weeks, my markers normalized and my mood followed. Data, decision, recovery. Not saying it's always that easy, but the more frequently we test, check in with ourselves, and consult the right practitioners, the more we give ourselves the opportunity to make small adjustments as opposed to doing complete overhauls years down the road.

Building Your "Executive Athlete Clinic"

Here's how I recommend assembling a bio-board of directors. You don't necessarily need them all at once, but having contact with each can be helpful depending on how your body changes over the years. Start with one. Build iteratively—like any scaling business.

- **Functional MD or ND (naturopathic doctor):** quarterback of labs and hormones
- **Chiropractor/body-mechanic:** posture, fascia, nervous-system flow. Look for DNS, ART, or FRC-certified pros.
- **Health Coach/Bio-Optimization Specialist:** bridges knowledge into habits. (Yes, NBHWC-certified coaches are worth it.)
- **Nutritionist (functional or sports):** micro-nutrient detective and gut strategist
- **Therapist or Breathwork facilitator:** mental hygiene is cellular hygiene.
- **Performance Lab:** think Next Health, Upgrade Labs, or Restore Hyper Wellness—IVs, cryo, red-light, ozone.

Alternative Insurance and Community Models

So, the bad news. Of all the biohacking tools I've used over the years, my insurance has covered next to zero percent. Traditional insurance rarely covers optimization. The goodish news? That's where new collectives step in. There is a growing awareness and real data to support that preventative care is the way to optimize health and that investing in our health early on leads to far better outcomes later in life. Collectives carry the same ethos and philosophy as biohacking itself: decentralize, personalize, empower. Below are some resources that are trying to change the game:

- **CrowdHealth:** a membership-based alternative to insurance; transparent pricing, community-funded bills, and direct doctor pay
- **Sedera Health and Zion HealthShare:** similar "cost-sharing" ecosystems; ideal for self-employed or entrepreneurial execs
- **Function Health and Health Savings Accounts:** often tax-deductible when used for diagnostics and prevention

Learning from the Masters

You don't have to reinvent the wheel; you just have to listen to the people building better wheels. I've spent the better part of the last fifteen years marinating myself in podcasts, wellness journals, white papers, books, and certifications to learn more about health, nutrition, and healthspan. I couldn't have done it without some of the amazing folks below, many of whom I consider to be personal gurus. You don't have to listen to all of them, but I recommend that you pick one or two and subscribe so that you're feeding yourself one or two hours a month of good content that keeps you up to date on topics that are particularly meaningful to you and your health.

Podcasts and Voices worth lending your ears:
- **Ben Greenfield Life:** the OG of human optimization
- **Myers Detox Podcast:** cutting-edge science for detoxing the body
- **Huberman Lab:** neuroscience meets daily ritual
- **The Doctor's Farmacy (Mark Hyman):** integrative medicine meets real food
- **The Human Upgrade with Dave Asprey**
- **The Genius Life with Max Lugavere**
- **MindPump:** fitness and workout optimization
- **Longevity with Nathalie Niddam:** OG biohacker at the fringe
- **The Cabral Concept with Dr. Stephen Cabral:** protocols made practical
- **Limitless MD with Puneet Sodhi:** peptides & longevity decoded
- **The Dr. Gabrielle Lyon Show**
- **Dr. Josh Axe Show**

Conferences & Events:
- **Biohacking Conference (by Dave Asprey):** LA, Miami, or Orlando rotation
- **Health Optimization Summit (London):** where data meets spirit

- **A4M Longevity Congress:** medical-grade anti-aging intel
- **Paleo f(x) and KetoCon:** nutrition and metabolism meccas

Books:
- *Super Human* by Dave Asprey
- *Total Gut Reset* by Dr. Lauryn Lax
- *From Sick to Superhuman"* by Matt Gallant and Wade Lighthearted

Crowdsourcing Wisdom

In the age of Reddit, Substack, and Threads, collective intelligence has become medicine's R&D department. Cutting through the noise is important, however, and the below are some credible ones to consider. Remember: cross-reference everything. Use the algorithm, don't become it. The internet is both oracle and illusion.

Smart communities:
- **r/Biohackers and Optimized Life Facebook Group:** protocol swaps minus the dogma
- **Substacks by Natalie Niddam, Kashif Khan, and Molly Eastman:** functional and feminine lens
- **The Collective (by Levels):** continuous-glucose tinkerers uniting data and dinner

Wearable Ecosystem:
- **WHOOP 5.0 / Apple Watch / Garmin / Fitbit / Google Pixel Watch:** wrist wearables for tracking health, recovery, strain, and sleep

- **Oura Gen 3 and Ultrahuman Ring Air:** biometric ring that tracks sleep stages, HRV, temperature and recovery
- **Eight Sleep Pod 3:** smart mattress that uses temperature modulation, biometric sensors to optimize rest and recovery
- **HeartMath:** syncs your heart-rate rhythm with breath and coherence
- **Sensate and Appollo Neuro:** chest mounted or wrist/ankle wearable that delivers low-frequency vibration to stimulate the vagus nerve
- **Elite HRV and Hanu:** subscription platforms that interpret heart-rate variability data and stress resilience in real time

Apps:
- **MyFitnessPal:** comprehensive food logging and macro-tracking with barcode scanning
- **Cronometer:** comprehensive food logging that includes micro-nutrient tracking to adjust supplementation based on gaps
- **Headspace:** guided meditation and mindfulness training
- **SnoreLab:** records and analyzes your nightly snoring
- **Gyroscope:** a full spectrum life-dashboard app that aggregates sleep, steps, nutrition, habits and generates insights
- **Biohackr Biohacking Tracker:** tracks supplements, protocols, symptoms, and metrics to create a personalized stack

The Mentor Model

Sometimes the fastest way to upgrade is to apprentice under someone who is already living the experiment. Early on in my health journey, I committed to several longevity programs that gave me a 360-degree perspective that was critical to evolving my understanding of myself and my bio-individuality. Here are several notable ones below you might consider:

- Ben Greenfield's coaching programs blend faith, science, and sweat.
- Boulder Longevity Institute brings cutting edge medical expertise to solve for optimum longevity.
- Dr. Stephen Cabral's Integrative Health Practitioner course offers practical certifications for bio-curious leaders.
- Dave Asprey's Upgrade Collective is biohacking school meets spiritual retreat.
- WellnessFX + Forward clinics offer concierge models for executives who want quarterly data and monthly accountability.

Story from the Floor
The Power of a Functional Dream Team

Last year, after an exhausting stretch of travel, my deep sleep tanked and HRV flatlined. Instead of pushing through, I called my functional MD and my nutrition coach. They suggested running at-home labs that would give me insight within a week. The results showed that my thyroid and several neurotransmitters were low. Sure enough, when

I went back to reconcile my lab results to my food tracking app, I saw that I had been undereating carbohydrates for three to four months, which was contributing to the issue. Eating low carb can be a great option, but it's important to routinely carb-cycle while doing it. Once I connected the dots, I increased my carbs by 40-50g, and mood and energy levels were back to normal.

Functional medicine and biohacking aren't fringe anymore; they are the future of optimized leadership.

Budgeting for Your Biology

Optimization isn't cheap—but neither is burnout. As I have repeatedly mentioned, our health is our #1 competitive advantage. Keeping ourselves optimized means that we can get 20 to 30 percent more out of every prospect call, every critical leadership meeting, and allows us to trust that we will be at our intellectual and energetic best. What's that worth? Below are some ranges for what you might expect as you begin thinking about how and where to invest in your healthspan journey. It's like a professional-development budget for your biology.

Category	Annual Range	ROI
Labs & Diagnostics	$400-$1,500	Awareness = prevention
Coaching / ND Consults	$1,000-$3,000	Accountability
Supplements & Peptides	$800-$2,500	Energy ROI

Category	Annual Range	ROI
Tech & Wearables	$300-$1,000	Feedback loop
Conferences & Education	$400-$2,000	Community + knowledge

Red Flags and Green Lights

Red Flags:

- "One-size-fits-all" supplement plans
- Practitioners who never order labs
- Anyone promising "detox in ten days"

Green Lights:

- Root-cause focus
- Collaborative mindset (MDs + NDs + coaches)
- Measurable metrics tied to behavior change

Functional medicine and biohacking aren't fringe anymore; they are the future of optimized leadership. We've all been guilty of outsourcing our health, because who doesn't like an "easy button"? But the truth is, your practitioner reads your labs—you live them. Every morning, check in with the OG metrics: breath, energy, gratitude.

The Sales Buddha's Corner
The Doctor Within

The Dalai Lama once said, "If you think you are too small to make a difference, try sleeping with a mosquito." Biology works the same way—tiny changes, massive ripple. The deeper truth of functional medicine isn't about supplements or protocols; it's about agency. When you learn to read your own labs, when you build a team aligned with your wholeness, you're no longer outsourcing wellness. You're co-creating it. The system isn't the savior. Awareness is. So listen. Partner with brilliance. Attend the conferences, run the panels, wear the ring, inject the peptide if it serves you. But never forget: the real healer lives beneath your skin, waiting for permission to lead. Breathe, measure, integrate, repeat.

9

Financial Hacks Building Fiscal Fitness for a Well-Lived Life

We can rattle off revenue numbers, quota attainment percentages, and pipeline conversion stats without blinking. We've mastered performance dashboards, forecasting, and territory management. Yet ask the same high performer what their net worth is … silence. Ask about their budget … confusion. Ask where they overspend when stressed … denial mixed with shame. No one talks about it at sales kickoffs, but everyone feels it, that quiet, relentless hum beneath the surface of quota season. The subtle tightening in your chest when you realize the quarter closes in twelve days. The "if I can close this deal, then I can breathe" loop that plays like background music in the subconscious of every sales professional. None of this is personal. It's cultural.

The sales profession trains us to chase the sprint, not build the system. We are praised for short-term heroics, not long-term planning. And while the upside of sales can be extraordinary, the volatility can be punishing if you don't have a plan. But here's the deeper biohacking truth no one ever told us: Financial health is nervous-system health. Money dysregulation is body dysregulation. Chronic money stress spikes cortisol. It tanks our sleep. It wrecks our HRV. It makes us more reactive, less creative, more desperate, and less strategic. When our bank accounts are spinning, our brains are spinning. The autonomic nervous system reads financial uncertainty as threat.

That's why this chapter exists: Not to tell you how to budget in a traditional sense, but to help you build a financial nervous system—a body-mind-money ecosystem that supports emotional resilience, performance, and your long-term freedom and health.

The Physiology of Money Stress

Let's drop into science for a moment. The American Psychological Association reports that 77 percent of adults cite money as their primary stressor. That level of chronic financial anxiety triggers:

- Elevated cortisol
- Reduced heart rate variability (HRV)
- Increased inflammation
- Impaired decision-making
- Shortened attention span
- Disrupted sleep patterns

Over time, the biological effects mimic overtraining syndrome, the same physiological exhaustion elite athletes experience when they push beyond recovery capacity. Think about that: Debt ages your cells. Stress about bills reduces cognitive flexibility. Budget chaos lowers your access to intuition and creativity, the very skills that drive excellence in sales. This is WHY you feel foggy when money is tight. Why you chase deals that aren't aligned. Why you force conversations that previously would have flowed with ease. Scarcity shrinks your ability to see possibility. Financial regulation is nervous-system regulation. Stability creates sovereignty. Wealth creates breadth—in thinking, acting, and being.

Story from the Floor
The $15,000 Lesson

I will never forget the moment my financial illusions came crashing down. It was my first true six-figure year. I was in my late twenties, confident, hungry, and convinced I had cracked the code. And like many young sales pros, I celebrated by upgrading … everything. New apartment. Designer bags. Gorgeous dinners out. The dopamine hits were constant and expensive. Then tax season arrived. I remember opening the envelope—yes, back then taxes still arrived by mail—and feeling the blood drain from my face. I owed way more than I'd saved. Which is to say: I had saved nothing. That month became the most anxious of my career. I was selling million-dollar deals yet felt more broke than I did at twenty-five. Income without intention is insecurity disguised as success. That experience is what eventually pushed me into the deeper work of understanding my relationship with money. Not the numbers, but the nervous system wiring beneath the numbers.

That's what this chapter intends to help you understand.

Step One: Get Honest About the High-Low Cycle

Sales is an emotional rollercoaster, and so is the cash flow that comes with it. Big commission month? You feel invincible. Dry quarter? You question everything. It's not your imagination. This volatility creates what psychologists call financial trauma: the learned belief that money is unpredictable and unsafe, no matter how much you earn. It's why so many high earners still feel broke. It's why some reps making $400k a year live with the same anxiety as they did at $70k. To break the cycle, start tracking patterns:

- How do you feel the week after a big close?
- How do you behave when commissions dip?
- Do you overspend when stressed? Underspend?
- In what ways does your relationship with money reflect how you value yourself?
- When do you feel most out of control with finances?
- Which purchases give you energy? Which drain it?

Awareness is the first wealth hack, because when you see your patterns, you can change them.

Step Two: Build Your Financial Nervous System

Your financial nervous system is the set of habits, structures, and automations that protect you from emotional decision-making. It is your wealth equivalent of a morning routine or a sleep protocol. Here are the basics:

1. Emergency Fund: 3-6 Months Minimum

Not sexy, but essential. This is your psychological exhale. Your buffer. Your ability to negotiate, pivot, or walk away.

2. Tax Fund: A Separate Account

Transfer a percentage of every commission check immediately so that this is covered. No touching. No exceptions.

3. Automatic Investments: Set and Forget

Whether it's:

- 401(k)
- Roth IRA
- Index funds
- Brokerage auto-contributions

Automate deposits the same way you automate bill pay. This is compounding with discipline.

4. Quarterly Expense Reviews

Annual reviews are too slow and the sales cycle moves fast, so your expense audit cycle should too. Automation is to money what breathwork is to stress; it regulates you when your emotions want to derail the plan.

Step Three: Redefine Wealth

Most people define wealth as "having more," but real wealth is time, energy, optionality. Freedom. Optionality is the superpower—the freedom to choose work, clients, projects, and life directions based on values, not survival mode. I once coached a top producer for our firm who made north of seven figures. On paper he was thriving. Inside? He was exhausted. Burned out. His health was suffering. He hadn't taken a true vacation in over three years. He didn't need more money, he needed margin. So, ask yourself the transformative questions:

- What am I buying that's costing me peace?
- What would enough actually feel like?
- If my energy were currency, where am I overspending?

Step Four: Build Your Financial Dream Team

Just as you've built a functional health team with doctors, nutritionists, coaches, and trainers, you need a financial performance team. Your wealth "ecosystem" should include:

- A fiduciary financial advisor who is paid to serve your interests, not sell you products
- A CPA or tax strategist—especially important for variable-income earners
- A money therapist or mindset coach to help unravel scarcity wiring, people-pleasing patterns, or avoidance behaviors
- A bookkeeper or virtual CFO if you own your own business or run a commission-heavy practice

Some platforms worth exploring:
- Facet Wealth
- Empower
- Altruist
- Bari Tessler or the Soul of Money Institute for deeper emotional work

You cannot out-earn emotional patterns that you refuse to examine, and your financial pit crew can help you break them.

Step Five: Optimize Your Money Environment

Just like circadian rhythms, finances respond to cues. Automate good behavior by automating your savings, your investments, and routine bill payments. Take a few hours on a weekend to declutter your digital world by unsubscribing from retail triggers, sales emails, and anything that encourages emotional spending. There are some good apps to support fiscal mindfulness:
- You Need A Budget (YNAB)
- Monarch Money
- Mint
- Qapital
- Rocket Money

Step Six: Convert Earning Energy into Legacy

Once you've stabilized, you get to expand. I call this the Four Phases of Financial Flow. Phases 1–2 regulate the nervous system. Phases 3–4 regulate the soul. When you reach phase 4, Significance, generosity becomes your new dopamine.

1. **Survival Mode:** Pay the bills. Reduce chaos.
2. **Stability:** Build the buffer. Automate the basics.
3. **Sufficiency:** Invest. Diversify. Grow.
4. **Significance:** Give. Create legacy. Compound meaning.

Story from the Floor
The ROI of Peace

One of the most successful sales executives I ever managed once described her most powerful financial hack, and it wasn't a spreadsheet or investment strategy. It was a Sunday night money meditation. Ten minutes. Hands on heart and stomach. Breathing deeply. Giving thanks for what was working. She said it shifted her entire nervous system from anxiety to agency. Same job, same pipeline, and same market as her peers, with way different outcomes. Gratitude changes your neurology. Neurology changes your decisions. Decisions change your deal flow.

> Broken brains can't brainstorm. Stressed bodies can't sell at their best. Regulated nervous systems close bigger deals.

Advanced Hacks: From Function to Freedom

Once your foundation is strong, explore upper-tier tools:

- **Wealthfront/Betterment:** automated investing for hands-free growth

- **Ellevest:** women-centered investing focused on alignment
- **CrowdHealth or Healthshares:** insurance alternatives that reduce financial bloat
- **ChooseFI or Mr. Money Mustache:** communities focused on freedom, not accumulation
- **Real estate, REITs, fractional investing:** asset growth without overextension

When Financial Health Feeds Physical Health

Money isn't just math; it's metabolism. When your finances stabilize, your body softens. Your shoulders drop. Your prefrontal cortex lights back up. The neuroscience on this is clear: Chronic scarcity activates the amygdala and suppresses the prefrontal cortex—the center of logic, empathy, and innovation. Translation? Broken brains can't brainstorm. Stressed bodies can't sell at their best. Regulated nervous systems close bigger deals. Financial wellness is a leadership skill. Imagine this alignment for yourself: Your labs and finances reviewed quarterly, supplements restocked and budget reviewed monthly, HRV and spending tracked daily. It's not micromanagement, it's coherence. When you track your internal environment (biomarkers) and your external environment (money) with equal curiosity, you create a holistic operating system.

Financial Wellness Stack

Domain	Hack	Why It Works
Mindset	Money gratitude journaling	Activates reward circuitry; lowers cortisol
Strategy	50/30/20 budgeting	Simple, sustainable, predictable
Behavior	Automatic transfers	Removes decision fatigue
Knowledge	One finance podcast/week	Gradual identity shift through education
Spirit	Tithing or giving	Reinforces abundance and flow

Podcasts worth adding:
- Afford Anything
- Money Guy Show
- I Will Teach You to Be Rich
- The Psychology of Money

Story from the Floor
The Deal That Taught Me Enough

Years ago, I chased a major deal that I thought would "fix everything." I overworked, over-strategized, and over-identified with the outcome. And when it didn't close, I was devastated. One week later, two smaller, beautifully aligned deals dropped into my pipeline easily, naturally, effortlessly. That's when I realized that abundance feels like alignment, not achievement. Money flows when your energy is clean. For the baseball fans out there, everything moved when *I stopped gripping the bat.*

The Sales Buddha's Corner
The Currency of Enough

Money, like breath, expands when you stop holding it too tightly. The Buddha taught that desire becomes suffering not because we want too much, but because we grasp too hard. We attach. We cling. We identify. Financial wellness is rhythm, not riches. Ask yourself:

- Why do I pick up the bar tab every weekend?
- Why do I buy the designer automobile?
- What am I trying to prove? And to whom?
- Where am I spending from fear instead of freedom?

There's NO shame in any of this. Awareness is the first currency of growth. Money is stored intention. Every dollar you earn, spend, save, invest, or give carries your energy. It is a reflection of who you are becoming, not just what you can afford. Budget like a biohacker. Invest like an artist. Spend like someone who trusts themselves. And give like someone who knows that generosity compounds. Because in the end, abundance isn't what's in your account ... it's how you feel when you open it.

10

Need Some Inspiration?

The Proof Is Always in the Practice

I've always believed the best evidence of transformation isn't found in a lab or a leadership seminar. It's found in the lives of real people who decided to stop running on fumes and start performing from flow. Over the years, I've been blessed with mentors who changed my perspective, and with colleagues, clients, and friends whose journeys continue to inspire me. As Winston Churchill is credited with saying, "Perfection is the enemy of progress." These stories aren't about perfection. They're about evolution. Each one began with exhaustion and ended in expansion.

The Sales VP Who Swapped Burnout for Biometrics

When I met Michael, he was the classic high-flyer: top producer at our firm, private equity deals on speed dial, and an HRV score probably hovering around 30. He joked about "living on espresso and adrenaline." Then his body quit cooperating. He was pushing forty, and in a one-on-one conversation, vulnerably disclosed that he was gaining weight no matter what he tried. He recently had his first ever series of anxiety attacks. I encouraged him to speak to a functional medicine practitioner to do some lab work and instigate a deep dive to determine what was going on.

Michael started small: first with sleep tracking on Oura, magnesium before bed, blue-light blockers, and a 9 p.m. digital sunset. Within two months, his deep sleep doubled. But the breakthrough came when he restructured his day like an athlete. Morning sunlight. Midday walk instead of another Zoom. Afternoon cold exposure instead of more caffeine. Six months later, he told me, "I thought I was losing it, but in looking back I can see that I just hadn't been giving myself the time to recover. Now I close fewer deals—but they're better ones. And I'm much nicer to work with now. Ha!" That's what sustainable performance looks like.

> The best evidence of transformation isn't found in a lab or a leadership seminar. It's found in the lives of real people who decided to stop running on fumes and start performing from flow.

The Rookie Sales Rep Who Built Confidence Through Chemistry

Then there's Tanya, a twenty-nine-year-old sales rep who lived on energy drinks and impostor syndrome. She came to me after reading one of my LinkedIn newsletters. Her biggest insight? "My mood swings weren't emotional—they were glycemic. A direct reflection of my unhealthy food choices throughout my day." She tested her glucose with a

Levels continuous blood glucose monitor and found huge post-lunch crashes. With her functional medicine practitioner, she rebalanced meals for steady energy—protein first, caffeine later, evening magnesium. Within weeks, her energy stabilized—and so did her numbers. She finished the quarter at 165 percent of quota, calm, and centered.

The Turnaround: From Sales Bro to Sales Sage

You might recognize Brian Underwood, founder of Ketō OS (Prüvit). His story is the modern archetype of transformation. He went from door-to-door grind culture to leading one of the most innovative nutrition companies in the world. Brian has spoken openly about how ketosis, fasting, and mindfulness rewired his leadership. "Biohacking saved my life. I started using my body as data, not a dumping ground." He now runs his company with recovery baked into the culture—meditation before meetings, HRV-based travel planning, and "no phone zones" during team dinners. Leaders like Brian show what happens when physiology and philosophy align.

The Executive Who Stopped Outsourcing Her Energy

One of my favorite stories is Tracy, a VP at a global consulting firm. She'd achieved everything—title, salary, reputation—but felt like a spectator in her own life. After a corporate wellness seminar, she signed up for a full lab panel through Function Health. Her hormones, vitamin D, and ferritin were all low. Within weeks of supplementing, adding morning light walks, and prioritizing sleep, her brain came back online. But what really changed was her relationship with herself. She started journaling each morning with a prompt I often use: "What does my body need from me today?" Her answer usually wasn't "another meeting." Six months later, Tracy said, "I feel like I went from constantly managing my stress in unhealthy ways to mastering my energy and focus."

The Sales Leader Who Biohacked Her Team Culture

When corporate Chief BD Officer Angela started coaching teams through burnout, she integrated breathwork and mindfulness into weekly huddles and invested in wearables for her team to track the impact. At first, her team thought it was "woo woo." Then productivity soared as people started noticing a difference in their focus and consistent energy throughout the day. She explained it beautifully in a podcast: "Sales isn't about pushing harder. It's about recovering smarter. When your reps feel safe, they will sell better." This is the future of leadership—where neuroscience meets empathy.

The Health Convert

One of my favorite transformations came from Jason, a forty-five-year-old sales director who used to roll his eyes at anything related to mindfulness and wellness that the company proposed. After his third ulcer scare, he finally listened. He started with basics: Oura tracking, daily breathwork, inputting his daily food intake into MyFitnessPal, and committing to two rest days a week that he actually honored. Within a year, he'd lost twenty-five pounds and normalized his blood pressure. He laughed, "My close rate didn't double, but my capacity did."

The Company That Made Wellness Its KPI

Inspiration doesn't just come from individuals. Some organizations are really committed to rewriting the playbook. Take HubSpot. Their "HubWell" program rewards employees for steps, mindfulness, and even sleep. Leadership reported a 30 percent reduction in burnout symptoms—and yes, a measurable bump in sales productivity. Or consider Salesforce's "B-Well" initiative, offering coaching, sleep tracking, and nutrition classes. These programs prove that when wellness becomes culture, performance becomes contagious. It isn't fluff; it's neuroscience-based strategy and the future of corporate performance.

The Athlete Turned Sales Executive

Then there's Olga Gvozdenovic, a former pro basketball player who transitioned into sales leadership. She once told me during a podcast, "I realized business wasn't that different from sports, except in sports, we take recovery seriously." She brought that recovery mindset into corporate life: team breathwork, structured rest, and even cold plunges before major pitches. Her team's close rates skyrocketed, not because they hustled more, but because they learned to oscillate between intensity and recovery.

The Biohacking Mom Who Reclaimed Her Focus

Stephanie was a regional sales manager and mother of two. Her turning point came when she caught herself replying to emails during bedtime stories. She decided her kids deserved a regulated mother, not just a successful one. She hired a nutrition coach, swapped late-night Netflix for red-light therapy and reading, and started micro-dosing cold exposure in the mornings. Three months later, she told me, "I stopped multitasking my life. Now I manage my energy and focus like revenue-with intention." Her kids call it "Mom's new superpower."

The Mentor Who Modeled Integration

Years ago, one of my early mentors quoted a terrific book to me, *The Body Keeps the Score* by Bessel van der Kolk (Viking, 2014). "Self-regulation depends on having a friendly relationship with your body. If you don't feel safe inside your body, you can't feel safe in the world." If the body keeps score, so does the bank account, the marriage, and the mind. The goal is to get them all playing the same game. He taught me that inspiration isn't in perfection, it's in transparency. Watching him rebuild his health through meditation and functional medicine after decades of corporate stress showed me that reinvention doesn't have an age limit. At 83-years-old, he now leads retreats for executives on "Holistic High Performance," blending breathwork, strategy, and storytelling.

Public Inspiration: The Giants We Can Learn From

There are many, many thought leaders proving this integration works:

- Ben Greenfield, who mixes endurance training with spirituality and longevity science
- Dr. Mark Hyman, who reversed chronic illness through functional medicine
- Tara Brach, PhD, who focuses on meditation, radical acceptance, emotional freedom
- Dave Asprey, who turned personal burnout into a global biohacking movement
- Dr. Andrew Huberman, Neuroscientist at Stanford, who translates cutting-edge neuroscience into practical tools for optimizing health
- Robin Sharma, who offers high performance routines plus spiritual grounding
- Tim Ferris, who specializes as a human optimization pioneer
- Natalie Niddam, who decodes peptides and performance for longevity

Every one of these experts demonstrates that high performance isn't a grind. It's a flow state built on cellular integrity and self-trust.

From Inspiration to Application

Every story here shares a pattern: Awareness. Small, measurable action. Long-term transformation. Biohacking isn't about extremes. It's about our feedback loops—physiological, emotional, and financial—that tell us when we're thriving and when we're off track. So, if you're reading this wondering where to start: Start with awareness. Your next breakthrough doesn't require a new product; it requires presence. Inspiration is remembrance. Every story that moves us reminds us of what's possible. These stories are impressive, but they're meant to activate us. They prove that the modern Sales Athlete isn't someone who has it all. It's someone who *integrates* it all.

The Sales Buddha's Corner
The Spark of Service

There's a quote I keep on my desk: "Be the person you needed when you were younger." Every transformation story in this chapter began with someone brave enough to get honest—about fatigue, fear, or finances—and then chose curiosity over shame. That's what this whole movement is about. It's not about biohacking our way to immortality. It's about remembering that when we change our internal chemistry, we can change our external world. When we are inspired, we perform better, we lead better, we live better.

11

Your Stack Is Your Superpower

Most of us don't grow up dreaming of a career in sales. There's no college major titled "Becoming a World-Class Sales Athlete," no neatly carved academic path that ushers us into this world of navigating clients, reading energy, chasing numbers, and building trust across boardrooms, industries, and time zones. Sales is one of the only professions where people arrive not by design, but by drift—by accident, by opportunity, by the subtle way life nudges us toward what we're naturally good at before we even realize it.

And because of that, it's been my experience that sales professionals can carry around a quiet insecurity: "I don't have a pedigree." It's an internal soundtrack most won't say out loud, but many feel. The sense of being "less than" in rooms where others have linear résumés, Ivy League degrees, or more formal titles. You may have felt it yourself— sitting across from a CFO who speaks in acronyms or presenting to a board where everyone seems to have letters after their names. But here's the truth most people never hear: *The fact that you didn't follow a straight line is not a limitation. It's an advantage.*

Sales, and leadership, are *human* professions. They reward curiosity, grit, emotional intelligence, adaptability, and lived experience more than they reward any textbook knowledge. They require you to understand people, not just products, to navigate complexity, not just spreadsheets, to move comfortably through ambiguity, not just structure. And the people who do that best? They are almost always the ones who didn't follow the predictable route.

If you've ever doubted your path, I want this chapter to be the moment that doubt dissolves. Because your path—your background, your lived experience, your story—is not something you need to overcome. It is your stack. It's the thing that makes you irreplaceable. Every skill you picked up in another job. Every city you moved to. Every setback that forced you to evolve. Every risk that stretched you. Every personal transformation—physical, emotional, spiritual. Every relationship, leadership lesson, heartbreak, reinvention, and breakthrough. *All of it* is part of your stack. And your stack is your superpower.

The more you recognize this, the more you stop apologizing for who you are, and instead start owning the immense value your lived experience brings to every room you walk into. When you walk into a meeting as your full self, not the self you think you're supposed to be, everything changes. You sell differently. You lead differently. You speak differently. You influence differently. Confidence stops being something you perform. It becomes something you embody. If you look closely at anyone you admire—an elite salesperson, a CEO, a founder, a board member, an exceptional leader—you'll notice something important: Their power didn't come from doing things "the right way." It came from the unique combination of experiences, failures, quirks, passions, and pivots that shaped how they see the world.

Your stack is exactly that—your personal combination of lived experiences, skills, curiosities, influences, beliefs, and lessons that no one else on Earth has in the same order, with the same intensity, and in the same timing. It's your story, but it's more than that. It's your lens. It's your operating system. It's the pattern of strengths you developed by living your life, not someone else's. Most people don't realize how valuable this is because your stack feels normal to you. You've lived inside it for so long that it becomes invisible. But to others—clients, prospects, colleagues, leaders—your stack is a rare blueprint. It's the source of your instinct, intuition, perspective, and insight.

Your stack is the thing that makes you interesting.

Your stack is the thing that makes you credible.

Your stack is the thing that makes you trustworthy.

Think about every chapter of your life so far: the job you took in your twenties that paid nothing but taught you everything; the manager who pushed you too hard and forced you to learn boundaries; the move to a new city where you didn't know anyone; the season when you were broke, scared, or overwhelmed; the moment you realized you could reinvent yourself; the heartbreak that cracked you open; the trip that changed your worldview; the health scare that forced you to prioritize your wellness;

the book or podcast that shifted your perspective; the year you decided to take your health seriously; the moment you stopped abandoning yourself.

Every experience added something to your stack—discipline, empathy, resilience, optimism, discernment, spiritual depth, courage, creativity, hunger, humility, or wisdom. And this is why two people can walk into the same room and have entirely different conversations with the same client. People feel you—not your résumé. They feel your depth, your lived truth, your energy.

This is why sameness is not persuasive. Sameness does not differentiate. Sameness does not build trust. People don't buy from robots. They buy from humans—humans who bring something real, lived, and honest. Here's the truth almost no one says out loud: The people who didn't follow a traditional path are often the strongest, most adaptable, most emotionally intelligent leaders in the room. Why? Because when your life has not been linear, you had to become the structure. You had to build your confidence through experience, not credentials. You had to learn how to read people, adapt quickly, listen deeply, and recover from setbacks. You had to create momentum without guarantees. You had to rely on instinct, not just instruction.

If your path has ever looked messy, nonlinear, late-blooming, unconventional, unpredictable, or "accidental," then hear this clearly: You are not behind. You are built differently. Sales, leadership, and business development are fields where straight lines can work against you. They create rigidity. They breed blind spots. They reward people who follow maps instead of people who can navigate without one. But life rarely gives maps. It gives us moments. It gives us pivot points. It gives us challenges that force us to evolve. It gives us detours that end up being the most important chapters we ever lived.

Those who traveled the winding path show up differently. They see nuance. They catch undercurrents. They sense energy shifts in a room. They anticipate objections before they're voiced. They handle personalities, politics, and pressure because their lives taught them how long before their careers ever needed them to. These are not weaknesses. These are assets. Your stack was built in the trenches of real life—and that makes it priceless.

This brings us to one of the deepest truths of performance: Most people move through their careers believing they have to fix themselves to become successful. They think confidence comes from eliminating flaws, smoothing out edges, or "improving weaknesses" until they resemble some imagined version of a perfect corporate citizen. But confidence doesn't come from perfection, it comes from integration. Stacked Living is the philosophy that your power grows by weaving every part of yourself into a coherent whole. Your experiences, your strengths, your quirks, your past selves, your reinventions, your emotional patterns, your physical practices, your risks, your failures, your identity shifts—they all live in one ecosystem. And the more integrated the system, the more powerful the human.

Neuroscience shows that people perform at their highest levels when their internal world is aligned—when the mind, body, and nervous system are communicating clearly. HRV improves when we live in coherence, when our values, actions, and identity point in the same direction. Your stack is not random chaos. It is the architecture of your coherence. When you stop dividing yourself—"this part of my life counts; this part doesn't"—your nervous system stops burning energy trying to reconcile competing identities. That freed energy becomes clearer intuition, stronger presence, steadier confidence, faster recovery, more creativity, better judgment, and deeper resilience.

This is also where the Sales Athlete lens becomes essential. You cannot have coherence without integrating your body, mind, emotional capacity, and leadership identity. Your physiology is not separate from your performance. Your mindset is not separate from your influence. Your recovery is not separate from your results. Your spiritual depth is not separate from your presence. Your workouts, your sleep, your breathwork, your recovery habits, your supplements all shape the energy you bring into every room. Your mental practices, your vision, your emotional intelligence, your intuition shape your leadership. Your experiences, your setbacks, your reinventions shape your compassion and your confidence. It's all one stack. One system. One integrated identity.

So how do you recognize and own your stack?

You start with the story that's not on your résumé. You identify your throughlines. You name your formative chapters. You integrate your practices. You craft your personal "stack narrative," the honest story of how you became the executive, professional, and leader you are. The story that roots your confidence in the truth of your lived experience. Most importantly, you live your stack out loud. You stop hiding. You stop apologizing. You stop editing

When you understand your stack, you stop trying to fit in. You start standing out.

yourself. You stop shrinking. You walk into rooms with the full strength of your story behind you, knowing that your uniqueness is not something to apologize for; it's something to leverage. *When you understand your stack, you stop trying to fit in.* You start standing out. And in sales, leadership, and life, standing out is the real competitive edge.

When you look back at your life, it's easy to see the detours, the challenges, the reinventions, and the unexpected turns as obstacles you had to overcome or things to regret or apologize for. But when you look at them through the lens of your stack, you begin to see something else: Every moment was preparing you. Every season was shaping you. Every chapter was giving you a unique strength you would later need. Your stack was not an accident. It was a curriculum. One you didn't sign up for but graduated from anyway, with more capacity, clarity, grit, empathy, and instinct than someone who followed a straight line ever could. This is why your story matters.

You are the competitive edge. When you understand your stack, you operate from depth. You show up as grounded instead of performative. You become someone people trust because your presence is congruent—clear, stable, integrated, and real. People respond to that in ways you cannot fake. There is something extraordinary that happens when you start showing up as your full self. You stop over-explaining. You stop auditioning. You stop trying to become someone else's idea of a leader. You start walking into rooms with a kind of ease that can't be faked. You start asking better questions. You start seeing relationships differently. You start negotiating from strength. You start shaping conversations, not chasing them. You become someone who influences through presence, not pressure.

If there is one message I want to leave you with in this final chapter, it's this: You are not here to be a copy of anyone. You are here to be the full expression of your stack, and your stack is brilliance.

Take everything you've learned in these chapters—about health, performance, recovery, leadership, identity, emotional intelligence, financial wellness, spirituality, and human potential—and let it all become part of your stack. Let it refine you. Let it guide you. Let it steady you. Let it elevate you. The highest version of you—the healthiest, strongest, clearest, most grounded version—is the one that understands you never needed to be perfect. You only needed to be you. Let the knowing of this open doors you once thought were beyond your reach.

The Sales Buddha's Corner
The Stack You Already Carry

The Sales Buddha reminds us:

We spend much of our early career trying to become someone. Later, if we are lucky, we realize that our real work is remembering who we've been all along.

Every success you chased, every rejection that stung, every detour, failure, reinvention, and risk was not a distraction from your path. It was the path.

Nothing was wasted.

The skills you learned when you were broke taught you resourcefulness.

The heartbreak taught you empathy.

The career pivots taught you adaptability.

The pressure taught you resilience.

The seasons you thought you were behind taught you patience.

Your life has been training you long before your title ever did.

Most people enter rooms trying to prove themselves, but the ones who truly influence enter rooms already knowing who they are.

The Sales Buddha does not try to erase their past selves. They integrate them.

They do not chase confidence. They build coherence.

They understand that performance is not just strategy or skill. It is energy. It is presence. It is alignment between body, mind, and purpose.

And they know the greatest competitive advantage is not found in becoming someone else, but is found in becoming fully yourself.

Because in business, in leadership, and in life, we are all athletes. And the strongest competitors are not those with perfect resumes, but those who learned to turn their entire journey into strength.

So walk forward knowing this: You were never behind. You were being built.

Your stack is not accidental. It is earned.

And your superpower was never something you had to find.

It is something you already carry.

Acknowledgments

As my great-grandmother used to say, "Sh*t makes great fertilizer." I've certainly had my share of it in life, and in many ways, this book grew from those messy, humbling, and transformative seasons. The lessons that challenged me most ultimately became the foundation for the ideas you'll find in these pages.

My deep thanks to my editor, Mark Leichliter, whose guidance helped shape this manuscript, to the incredibly talented designer P. J. (Tricia) Hoover, and to marketing guru Seharut Suankeow for helping bring this vision into the world.

A mentor once asked me, "What do you need to let go of to become the vessel for the impact you're meant to have?" This book exists in part because friends, colleagues, and teammates cared enough to be honest with me about my blind spots, pushing me to grow in ways that weren't always comfortable but were always necessary. I'm equally grateful to the community of biohackers, health seekers, and lifelong learners whose curiosity and generosity continually inspire me.

I'm blessed to be surrounded by extraordinary thinkers, kind souls, and generous hearts. My tribe of brilliant, patient humans has become my chosen family, and I'm endlessly grateful they continue to support me, challenge me, and cheer me on.

If this book offers even one reader a new perspective on their health, performance, or potential, then the journey was worth it. My hope is that the lessons I learned, often the hard way, help someone else avoid a few pitfalls and move faster toward their own version of holistic success. Because in business, in life, and in leadership, we are all athletes, and our health is the foundation that makes everything else possible.

About the Author

Nicole Ward is Senior Vice President of Sales at Aon, host of the Aon at the Top and Executive Athlete podcasts, and founder of the Executive Athlete platform.

She is a performance strategist, biohacker, and health nerd working at the intersection of leadership, physiology, and conscious power. Nicole is a National Board Certified Health & Wellness Coach (NBHWC), is currently completing her Master of Science in Nutrition Sciences at Tufts University, and will be a Certified Personal Trainer through the National Academy of Sports Medicine (NASM) in September 2026.

With more than two decades in executive leadership, Nicole brings boardroom credibility together with cutting-edge science in functional medicine, longevity, and autonomic nervous system optimization. Her work focuses on helping high-impact leaders restore coherence between their biology and their responsibilities so decisions, influence, and outcomes are driven by clarity rather than chronic stress.

Through her writing, speaking, and advisory work, she trains leaders to think, recover, and lead like elite athletes, building sustainable performance, emotional intelligence, and embodied presence in the environments where the stakes are highest.

Visit Nicole's website at:
www.nicoleelizabethward.com

For interviews, collaborations, or speaking engagements, email Nicole at:
nicole@nicoleelizabethward.com

To listen to the Executive Athlete Podcast, visit Nicole on YouTube at:
https://www.youtube.com/@nicolewardpodcast

Find Nicole online at:
LinkedIn: https://www.linkedin.com/in/nicoleward111/
TikTok: @nicole.ward111
Instagram: @nicoleward111

www.ingramcontent.com/pod-product-compliance
Lightning Source LLC
Chambersburg PA
CBHW071339150726
47997CB00002B/796